Better Principals,
Better Schools

A volume in
Urban Education Studies Series
Nicholas D. Hartlep, *Series Editor*

Better Principals, Better Schools

What Star Principals Know, Believe, and Do

edited by

Delia Stafford
The Haberman Educational Foundation, Inc.

Valerie Hill-Jackson
Texas A&M University

INFORMATION AGE PUBLISHING, INC.
Charlotte, NC • www.infoagepub.com

Library of Congress Cataloging-in-Publication Data

A CIP record for this book is available from the Library of Congress
http://www.loc.gov

ISBN: 978-1-68123-364-2 (Paperback)
       978-1-68123-365-9 (Hardcover)
       978-1-68123-366-6 (ebook)

Printed in the United States of America

Dr. Martin Haberman
(1932–2012)

The attributes of star principals, which make them effective against all odds and in spite of irrational pressures, are more than behaviors. They are behaviors undergirded by an ideology. The ideology and behaviors are interwoven; they are of a piece. The connection between what star principals do and how they think about what they do cannot be broken.... Star principals are doers and thinkers.

—Dr. Martin Haberman
Star Principals Serving Children in Poverty (Kappa Delta Pi, 1999)

CONTENTS

About the Series ix

Foreword xi

Prologue: A Star Principal for Every School.................................... xiii
Delia Stafford and Valerie Hill-Jackson

1   Principal Netzer and the Tale of Two Urban High Schools.............. 1
    Gus Jacob and Jennifer Waddell

2   No Principal Left Behind? The Core Beliefs of Nine Urban
    Elementary Principals in a Midwest School District
    Implementing No Child Left Behind 15
    Rodney E. Watson and Valerie Hill-Jackson

3   The Other Side of the Desk: The Beliefs and Behaviors
    of Star Principals at Turnaround Schools 37
    Jim Robins

4   Staffing Urban Principals in an Era of Hyper-Reform: A Case
    from "The Port of Good Things"... 49
    Myra I. Whitney and Beverly E. Cross

5   The Case for Selecting Better Principals... 63
    Valerie Hill-Jackson and Delia Stafford

About the Editors 81

About the Contributors.. 83

ABOUT THE SERIES

The *Urban Education Studies* book series was created to share the lives and voices of educators, students, and parents connected to urban areas. In concert with the authors, we seek to extend our audiences' understandings of events, perceptions, and practices that directly and indirectly relate to issues of race, gender, socio-economic status, hetero-normativity, and other issues of social subjugation that impact students and families. We are committed to increasing the visibility of urban issues from the perspectives and documented experiences of the people most affected by them, in order to continue and begin conversations on issues of equity and equality in complex urban contexts.

What we hope to bring new to publications of equity and equality in diverse racial contexts, are more complex analyses of peoples' lived experiences, implications for policies and practices in urban school settings, moments of joy, and slivers of hope for the future success of children of color and children disenfranchised by poverty and social oppression. It is not our intention to repeat well-worn conversations about educators and urban families in ways that re-instantiate dominant ideologies and the *status quo*. Rather, we wish to publish texts with new lenses, new quandaries, and innovative questions, which reflect societal change *and* ongoing struggles for justice. In this series, we not only challenge stock stories and majoritarian tales, but traditional ways of thinking and constructing answers to the persistent questions plaguing urban stakeholders. We invite our audience to engage with us as we present innovative methods, conceptual designs, and methodologies focused on emic and etic research designs of equity and equality, with the goal to enhance our knowledge of and compassion for the numerous realms of people thriving and surviving in rich urban settings.

The second book in our series comes from editors Delia Stafford and Valerie Hill-Jackson. *Better Principals, Better Schools: What Star Principals Know, Believe, and Do* focuses on the knowledge, beliefs, and actions of effective K–12 school principals. These "star" principals have an ideology that undergirds their effectiveness at serving children in poverty. As Haberman states, "The attributes of star principals which make them effective against all odds and in spite of irrational pressures are more than behaviors. They are behaviors undergirded by an ideology" (p. x). There is a need for more research in urban contexts that focuses on leadership practices rather than teachers and/or students. Stafford and Hill-Jackson's book contributes much to this effort.

Nicholas D. Hartlep, PhD
Illinois State University
Series Editor

Thandeka K. Chapman, PhD
University of California, San Diego

Kenneth Fasching-Varner, PhD
Louisiana State University
Series Co-editors

REFERENCE

Haberman, M. (1999). *Star principals serving children in poverty.* Indianapolis, IN: Kappa Delta Pi.

FOREWORD

Having served as a long time educator, it is rare indeed to find individuals that commit a lifetime of service to the children and youth of America, especially for the large numbers of children in poverty. I feel fortunate to have found one such person, Dr. Martin Haberman distinguished professor, emeritus (1932–2012). With his research and consistent philosophy I have witnessed firsthand, I know that he made a remarkable difference for thousands of students all across the USA.

The ongoing work at the Haberman Educational Foundation, Inc. (HEF) continues to make his research available to school districts nationally. His life-long vision, in terms of selecting the right individuals that teach, as well as the appropriate school leaders to manage the challenge, is tethered to a dream for every student to have the opportunity to reach their full potential. Dr. Haberman's search for indicators of an individual's core beliefs regarding instruction and connecting with students would be hard to match. His research spans 50 years and the Star Teacher and Star Principal interviews are being used across the states on a very broad scale. Districts where I have served, beginning in 2004 to the present, have used the research based interviews; I am a sincere advocate for what he has contributed to the education world.

Dr. Haberman's scholarship on leadership selection is proving prophetic and his bountiful body of research will have a lasting effect if we, as educators, continue to spread the story of his life's work. This publication is a tribute to an academic icon, Dr. Haberman, who is more than deserving of the recognition. He was a husband, a father, and a kind and generous man who had a singular obsession; for every individual willing and ready

Better Principals, Better Schools, pages xi–xii
Copyright © 2016 by Information Age Publishing

to learn to experience a better future—for the adults and youth in every city and every school. May he rest in peace as we move his dream along the highway of life, liberty and the pursuit of happiness; nothing would have thrilled him more!

I am humbled to give testimony to his great and lasting legacy.

—Dr. Terry Grier
Superintendent, Houston Independent School District
Recipient of the Green-Garner Award
2014 Urban Educator of the Year

PROLOGUE

A STAR PRINCIPAL FOR EVERY SCHOOL

Delia Stafford
Valerie Hill-Jackson

Schools are only as good as their principals. This modest adage sums up five decades of Dr. Martin Haberman's (1932–2012) research; he spent his career improving the life chances of underserved learners with studies fixated on selecting the right leaders to support them. Haberman was one of the most prolific scholars on school administrators of the twentieth and twenty-first centuries to date. He characterized 'star principals' as school leaders who succeed in the most desperate school environments in spite of the bureaucratic restraints set in motion against them by state and school district mandates. Haberman calculated that effective urban school districts are non-existent because all large school systems are failing to some degree. Yet, within every one of these school districts there are highly effective schools. All of us absorbed by processes to scale-up the numbers of indispensable leaders are interested in knowing 'why are some principals successful while others struggle to turnaround their schools?' Despite the tome of literature on effective school leadership for improved student performance (Brewer, 1993; Damon, Martorell, & Rockoff, 2009; Dhuey & Smith, 2014; Eberts & Stone, 1988; Grissom, Kalogrides, & Loeb, 2014; Hallinger & Heck, 1998;

Better Principals, Better Schools, pages xiii–xviii
Copyright © 2016 by Information Age Publishing

Leithwood, Louis, Anderson, & Wahlstrom, 2004; Witziers, Bosker, & Kruger, 2003) and the various calls to action to improve the hiring selection process (Rammer, 2007) and evaluation (NAESP & NASSP, 2012) of principals, the field of educational leadership remains ill-equipped in identifying quality principals on a mass scale or for an entire school district.

For those who ask, 'yeah, but *how* do you create better schools and what does *better* look like?' this volume answers these questions. The thesis of *Better Principals, Better Schools: What Star Principals Know, Believe, and Do* is simple: a star principal thinks, feels, and acts in effective ways that set him/her apart from the average school CEO. Haberman, in *The Leadership Functions of Star Principals Serving Children in Poverty*, proposed a new portrait of millennium school leaders that is worth repeating at length:

> Tomorrow's urban principal will not be able to function as the building manager of a traditional school. Any individual with such narrow perceptions and behaviors will be overwhelmed by district mandates, by the expectations of the public, community and parents, and by the exploding knowledge base regarding how and what children should learn. To be successful, tomorrow's principal will be required to function as the leader of a major non-profit community-based learning organization. The challenge will be selecting and preparing futurists who were themselves educated in the past. . . . As the 21st century dawns, the role of the school—particularly the urban school—has been completely transformed. . . . Using any reasonable criteria (student achievement, graduation rate, preparation for higher education, preparation for the world of work, safety, creativity, attendance, service to the community, development of individual skills and talents, citizenship, preparation for life in a multicultural and global society, or the development of internal motivation to function as a lifelong learner) no urban school district can demonstrate that it is delivering on its own stated goals. (Haberman, 2001, Introduction, p. 2)

Haberman insists that the twenty-first century administrator must evolve from white collar administrators into community workers due to the expanding responsibilities associated with the job. Also, the demographic mandate dictated by the increasing diversity among K–12 students requires a school leader who can meet the needs of various marginalized learners. This type of futurist school leadership must be creative and adapt to the mutating demands of local political, social, and educational environments—and the neo American learner—concurrently.

Haberman (1999) proposes 11 mid-range functions (beliefs and behaviors) for administrators: (1) leadership; (2) commitment to student learning; (3) theory into practice; (4) role of the school serving students in poverty; (5) curriculum and instructional leadership; (6) creating a positive school climate and fighting burnout; (7) evaluation/accountability; (8) decision making; (9) fallibility; (10) administrative style; and (11)

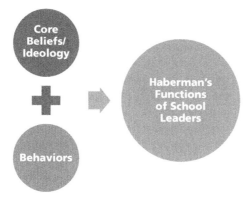

Figure P.1 Haberman's 11 Core Functions (dispositions) as a product of school leaders' beliefs and behaviors.

administrative relations with parents and community (see Chapter 5 of this volume). Figure P.1 demonstrates the way in which one's core beliefs are tethered to behaviors. Quite simply, the behaviors of school leaders is an indication of the way they think. Haberman explains that the behavior of school leaders has influences beyond state mandates, training, and leadership standards. Upon closer scrutiny, we learn that school leadership behavior is dictated by their ideology or beliefs; as one believes, one does. Haberman enlightens,

> The attributes of star principals, which make them effective against all odds and in spite of irrational pressures, are more than behaviors. They are behaviors undergirded by an ideology. The ideology and behaviors are interwoven; they are of a piece. The connection between what star principals do and how they think about what they do cannot be broken. In other words, educators who believe they can learn the "magic" behaviors without having the belief system that goes with it are wasting their time. Conversely, those who would assume that, because they agree with the ideology, they can automatically perform as star principals are equally deluded. Star principals are doers and thinkers. (Haberman, 1999, pp. x–xi)

Those who read *Better Principals, Better Schools* will recognize that all school leaders exhibit Haberman's 11 core functions in some form or fashion.

However, these 11 dispositions are employed differently by stars because they have a belief system—backed by a commitment to social justice—which lies in stark contrast to their underachieving peers. Stars believe that their effort, on behalf of underserved students, may mean the difference between life (a sound education, quality employment opportunities, contributions to society, etc.) and death (drop-out, under/no employment, drugs, jail, demoralized outlook, etc.). Star principals have a dream for their students' lives that transcends adequate yearly progress and test scores, but looks down the road for ways to improve learners' life chances and uplift the local school community. The National School Board Association's report, *Which Way is Up: What the Research Says about Turnaround Strategies*, mimics this assertion and inform, "Most studies conclude that principals and teachers have the most impact on student achievement" (Center for Public Education, 2013, p. 2). The core beliefs of stars guide uncompromising leadership behavior, which translates to student achievement as well as positive interactions and relationships with all stakeholders in the community for the short and long-term.

The editors of this book appealed to several scholar-practitioners who are equally as passionate and well versed on the star principal functions. For those who ask, 'yeah, but what do effective leadership at turnaround schools look like?' the contributors in this volume show us by sharing accounts that demonstrate what star principals know, believe, and do. The editors bookend the conversation with the prologue that shares the rationale for this volume and chapter five, which makes a case for selecting star principals. But the case examples begin in *Better Principals, Better Schools* with chapter one as Gus Jacob and Jennifer Waddell reveal two school makeovers made by one stellar principal. In chapter two, Rodney Watson and Valerie Hill-Jackson unveil the voices of nine urban elementary principals who wrestle with the chaotic world of reform for No Child Left Behind in environments with limited resources and even less guidance for school leaders. They assess how these principals withstand the pressures of high stakes mandates as their core beliefs are tested. Meanwhile in chapter three, Jim Robins discloses two intimate portraits of star principals who demonstrate two of Haberman's 11 core-functions with dedication and conviction. In the fourth chapter, Myra Whitney and Beverly Cross release some promising strides in staffing for the city of Memphis, in *The Port of Good Things*, using the Haberman Principal Pre-Screener.

> These disparate cases converge to propose the same idea that underperforming schools can and should be "turned around" inserts a level of urgency, energy, and hopefulness into a longstanding professional conversation dominated, until recently, by the much more guarded language of "school improvement." The turnaround concept prods us to confront failure head on and to accept responsibility for "making things right"—not at some vague time in the distant future, but soon. This concept is also the practical face of efforts to achieve equitable outcomes for students in our schools. . . . Evidence, mostly from non-school organizations, portrays leadership as the major factor accounting for successful turnarounds. (Leithwood & Strauss, 2009, pp. 2–3)

The principals at these turnaround schools are advocates, users or exemplars of the Haberman selection process; all of whom directed their schools from underperforming to successful. Star principals convey certainty that their teachers can improve student performance and that the students, with the right support, are capable of learning. Aspirations of high student achievement are almost always at the forefront of their planning and action. Star principals set explicit operational goals regarding students' academic performance, which are clearly communicated to school stakeholders (Brown & Green, 2014).

Haberman's core functions come to life with the narratives of star principals and we arrive at a closer understanding as to why some leaders succeed in turning around schools while others fail. With nearly five decades of Haberman's theories buttressed by practice, it would be impossible to produce a volume which is fully representative of all of Haberman's accomplishments among leaders, or that can adequately address the entire list of core functions for talented principals. In chapters one through four we aim to bring to the attention of a wider audience a selection of star principals and school districts, whose uncelebrated work in their schools, has yielded improvement for students and teachers. These chapters are intended to ignite critical reflection for readers and operationalize (a) the orientation of social justice leadership; and (b) the functions of 'star' principals.

Anyone who is keenly focused on the development or selection of principals will find these stories of star principals more than stimulating and thought-provoking, but exemplars worth modeling for a national shift in hiring practices—with the hope of ensuring *a star principal for every school.*

REFERENCES

Brown, A., & Green, R. L. (2014). Practices used by nationally blue ribbon award winning principals to improve student achievement in high-poverty schools. *National Forum of Applied Educational Research Journal, 27*(1/2), 2–18.

Brewer, D. J. (1993). Principals and student outcomes: Evidence from U.S. high schools. *Economics of Education Review, 12*(4), 281–293.

Center for Public Education. (2013). *Which way is up?: What the research says about turnaround strategies.* National School Board Association. Retrieved from http://www.centerforpubliceducation.org/Main-Menu/Policies/Which-Way-Up-At-a- glance/Which-Way-Up-Full-Report.pdf

Damon, C., Martorell, P., & Rockoff, J. (2009). *School principals and school performance.* Working Paper No. 38. Washington, DC: The Urban Institute.

Dhuey, E., & Smith, J. (2014). *How school principals influence student learning.* IZA Discussion Paper No. 7949. Retrieved from http://hdl.handle.net/10419/93329

Eberts, R. W., & Stone, J. A. (1988). Student achievement in public schools: Do principals make a difference? *Economics of Education Review, 7,* 291–299.

Grissom, J. A., Kalogrides, D., & Loeb, S. (2014). Using student test scores to measure principal performance. *Educational Evaluation and Policy Analysis,* Retrieved from http://epa.sagepub.com/content/early/2014/03/10/0162373714523831

Haberman, M. (1999). *Star principals serving children in poverty*. Indianapolis, IN: Kappa Delta Pi.

Haberman, M. (2001). *The leadership functions of star principals serving children in poverty*. Houston, TX: The Haberman Educational Foundation.

Hallinger, P., & Heck, R. H. (1998). Exploring the principal's contribution to school effectiveness: 1980–1995. *School Effectiveness and School Improvement, 9*(2), 157–191.

Leithwood, K., Louis, K. S., Anderson, S., & Wahlstrom, K. (2004). *How leadership influences student learning* (Report). Minneapolis, MN: University of Minnesota, Center for Applied Research and Educational Improvement.

Leithwood, K., & Strauss, T. (2009). Turnaround schools: Leadership lessons. *Education Canada, 49*(2). Retrieved from http://www.ceaace.ca/sites/default/files/EdCan-2009-v49-n2-Leithwood.pdf

National Association of Elementary School Principals (NAESP), & National Association of Secondary School Principals (NASSP). (2012). *Rethinking principal evaluation*. Washington, DC: Author.

Rammer, R. A. (2007). Call to action for superintendents: Change the way you hire principals. *The Journal of Educational Research, 101*(2), 67–76.

Witziers, B., Bosker, R. J., & Krüger, M. L. (2003). Educational leadership and student achievement: The elusive search for an association. *Educational Administration Quarterly, 39*(3), 398–425.

CHAPTER 1

PRINCIPAL NETZER AND THE TALE OF TWO URBAN HIGH SCHOOLS

Gus Jacob
Jennifer Waddell

CHAPTER OBJECTIVES

The learner will

1. Connect with a powerful story of how one principal, guided by the work of Dr. Martin Haberman, changed the landscape of two urban high schools in the Midwest;
2. Discover the powerful effects of selecting the right teachers;
3. Reflect upon his/her own experiences in hiring and guiding teachers in urban schools, and;
4. Hear from teachers about their experience with the Haberman Star Teacher Selection Interview.

At a symposium of the American Educational Research Association in 2002, Haberman asserted that in "preparing teachers for diverse children in poverty selection is more important than training." He added that, "...selection is 80% of the matter."

Better Principals, Better Schools, pages 1–14

This chapter tells the story of an urban high school principal who shares Dr. Haberman's belief and has put it into action. The principal has studied Haberman's work since the early 1990s. The chapter describes the ways in which the principal, Dr. Greg Netzer, has exemplified the work of Dr. Haberman's Star Teachers (2005) and star principals through the transformation of two urban high schools.

The first school, Washington High School, was the school at which Netzer's first assumed the role of high school principal. Taking over as principal in 2003, Netzer quickly discovered the need and the power of selecting the "right" teachers. The second school, Van Horn High School, by state legislative action, was annexed from a failing urban school district to become a part of a neighboring district. In 2008, the acquiring school district hired Netzer to lead the charge of reforming education and providing the school's students of poverty an opportunity for quality education. Consequentially, he seized the opportunity to hire the entire staff using Dr. Haberman's process of selecting teachers. This process (Haberman Star Teacher Selection Interview, 1994) laid the foundation for the restart of this failing school.

Dr. Haberman's work, immortalized through the actions of an exemplary urban school principal has molded two previously failing high schools into successful schools where principals and teachers universally share the belief that the success of all students is their responsibility. Through his work as principal of these schools, Dr. Greg Netzer has exemplified the work of Dr. Haberman. Told through the eyes of an esteemed colleague based on interviews with Netzer and select teachers, this chapter tells Netzer's story.

HOW IT ALL STARTED

In 1993, a colleague handed Greg Netzer an article authored by Dr. Martin Haberman (1991) entitled, "The Pedagogy of Poverty Versus Good Teaching." In constant search for improvement of teaching, and working with a group that provided professional development for schools in the Kansas City area, Dr. Netzer was very willing to look at something he had not seen before and something written by someone he did not know.

Netzer was convinced that this article was different from all he had studied. Haberman was talking about ideas different from those approached and spoken by others. He was talking about engagement by teachers who believed in kids. He was discussing ideas counter to what we see in failing schools, schools where teachers force compliance and use the traditional practices. These traditional classroom practices essentially define the "pedagogy of poverty" occurring in schools serving poor students and students of color. As Haberman (1991) notes, the pedagogy of poverty includes "giving information, reviewing tests, asking questions, assigning homework, giving directions, making assignments, monitoring seatwork... giving grades" (p. 290). But, in this article, Haberman (1991) was digging deeper and talking about something different, he was talking about reforming this pedagogy of poverty and he was eliciting conversation about what was possible for teachers in urban schools, "building environments, providing experiences, and then eliciting responses that can be reflected on" (Haberman, 1991, p. 291).

Netzer's excitement from reading the article and sharing it with many of his colleagues resulted in a phone call to Dr. Haberman. Netzer wanted to pursue, at a deeper level, the thinking of this educator who seemed to have answers others did not. When Netzer called Dr. Haberman, he was surprised that Dr. Haberman answered his own phone and was willing to visit with this unknown caller. Netzer shared how intrigued he had had been when reading the article; the answers he found in this article and the sophistication of the thinking written on these pages intrigued and inspired him. Netzer proceeded to ask, "Have you written anything else?" The response from the other end of the phone was quick and to the point, "Obviously, you aren't reading. I have been writing like this for over 20 years."

Netzer's excitement by what he had found was not dampened, yet with the awkwardness of this moment, the phone call ended quickly. Still in awe of what Haberman had written, the quest began to find more of this man's thinking. Netzer quickly discovered an article in *Education Week* (Gursky, 1992) written about Dr. Haberman entitled "Professor Predicts Urban Teachers' Success." This article revealed that not only had Haberman been writing about what makes a successful teacher for poor students and students of color in urban schools, but he had developed a selection interview that had been in use for 20 years. In Dr. Haberman's words, "The interview has proved almost flawless at predicting would-be teachers' professional potential in the classroom" (Gursky, 1992).

Netzer reflected on the article by Gursky, recalling that it "opened the door" and changed his thinking about the possibilities for good teaching. He was reading about concepts like persistence, believing teachers are the answer, and not loving kids, but *teaching* them. It also opened the door to the possibility that the complex and often nebulous task of identifying great teachers could actually be accomplished. Haberman's instrument was more than just that, "in your gut you know this is a person you want in your school." There were answers, and Haberman had constructed an interview that could help principals find those star teachers in a world where it appeared there are so few.

Netzer had worked as a former Social Studies Teacher, a high school principal in a small district near Kansas City, and had served as an educational consultant. Shortly after his exchange with Dr. Haberman (the less than comfortable but inspiring phone call), Netzer was hired by the Kansas City, Kansas School District to fill the role of Director of Instruction. While working as the Director of Instruction, Netzer had the opportunity to meet Dr. Haberman a couple of times. A colleague who worked at a Kansas City area university and facilitated a principals' institute invited Dr. Haberman to consult to the work. Netzer was invited to a couple of these dinner meetings. Netzer recalls his reaction to meeting Haberman in stating,

> I was sitting at the table with one of the brightest, most articulate individuals about urban education that exists. When I heard him say that 3,000 students drop out of high school every day and nobody cares, I knew he was willing to deal with the cold hard truth of a failing system that has become the norm, the expected in this country. It is an indictment of the education profession that we are in this condition.

Years later, when that role was no longer a part of the district's planned organizational structure, Netzer returned to high school administration, this time in the school where he had started his teaching, Washington High School in the Kansas City, Kansas School District.

TRANSFORMATION #1: WASHINGTON HIGH SCHOOL

Taking over as principal of Washington High School in Kansas City, Kansas in the fall of 2008, Netzer started experiencing what he recalls as the typical 25% annual turnover of teachers. His thoughts immediately turned to Dr. Haberman, to the articles Haberman had written, the conversations they had shared, and the selection instrument Haberman had developed. Until now, while knowing a lot about the work of Dr. Haberman, Netzer had not been trained to use the Haberman STAR Teacher Interview. Thus, year after year, he would spend the spring interviewing teachers, using what he thought were good questions, yet Netzer would spend the next spring replacing another 25% of his teachers. Netzer attributed much of this attrition to the fact that he was hiring the wrong teachers; they would leave or he would need to release them after a year or two of failed classroom performance. In Netzer's words, "I couldn't continue doing this... If the goal is to improve a school, you have to have a team that persists over time in serving some of the young people who need it most."

When the opportunity to attend the Haberman STAR Interview training was offered to Netzer in 2003, Netzer immediately seized the opportunity. Now equipped with a tool that brought, by this time, 30 plus years of research and practice, Netzer's goal was to improve the teaching staff of this high school. Identifying the right people was key in starting the renewal of Washington High School.

In 2003, Washington High School was a failing school, according to state AYP (Adequate Yearly Progress) status. The school did not make AYP; the graduation rate in 2002 was 74% and, in 2003, only 38% of the students were proficient or above in reading, only 8% were proficient in math. The school served a diverse group of students: 72% students of color, 38% White students and nearly 60% "economically disadvantaged" according to the State of Kansas (Kansas State Department of Education, 2013a, p. 1).

Selection of the right teachers became Netzer's priority. He felt that having the right teachers, "star teachers," would make his focus on instruction the norm, and would give the school a way of succeeding. This was a big challenge in a school that had a long history of failure. Yet, within five years of using the Haberman Star Teacher Selection Interview to hire his teachers, the school's proficiency levels had reached 72% in reading and 62% in math (Kansas State Department of Education, 2013b). Netzer recalls that, of the five high schools in the district, the only school scoring higher was the high school that was the academic magnet. The comprehensive high school that had a history of being celebrated as a success in the district had now fallen behind Washington High School in its academic level of achievement.

As Netzer reflected on what was happening, the most substantial change in his practices as principal was in his selection practices. He was now using this amazing tool developed by Martin Haberman. In reflecting on that time, Netzer stated,

> I found people I couldn't let out the door. It wasn't about credentials; it's about what kind of people they were. For the first time teachers who had a choice of high schools to go to were choosing Washington. The good candidates were saying that the questions that the principal asked were different and that "drew me to the school." In hindsight, I actually hired some that did not score very well on the interview because the pool of candidates seemed to be so shallow. I paid the price.

> After I was more confident with the prediction value of the interview, I remember refusing to hire a teacher that everyone in the district believed I should hire. After the interview, because of his answers on the interview, I refused to hire him. Everyone was amazed. Interestingly, after I left Washington, he was hired. He didn't last a year. After a couple of years of using Haberman's interview I knew there was a way of finding teachers who didn't give up on kids. Then it starts to change the culture when you start finding these teachers and they start talking to each other. So it not only tells you who to hire, but it also tells you who you do not want in your school.

> One of my favorite interviews was with the instrumental music teacher. If I would have used my traditional "made up" interview I would not have hired this young kid. But when he answered hard questions about serving at risk youth I knew I had something. I can remember asking him what we could do

about all of the at risk students. He looked me straight in the eye and said, "My program." Kids were drawn to him like a magnet and, yes his program, his band and instrumental program, made the difference for a lot of young people at our school. He wasn't the easiest person to have on staff. He wasn't always at work on time in the morning, but he believed in kids. I agree with Dr. Haberman, I don't think we can teach someone to believe in kids. They come with that.

In his continued attempt to improve the teaching staff at his school he could see that the candidates he was selecting were different. They weren't always the most energetic, the most attractive, or the most skilled. But they had something others did not; they had the potential of serving urban students better. They had beliefs and values that kept them from blaming students for failure. They were determined in finding ways to meet the needs of students who were highly at-risk, students who had been underserved by our schools and had previously experienced few opportunities for school success. Without effective teachers, star teachers, as Dr. Haberman called them, there was little hope.

Netzer could see that interviewing with this well-studied instrument provided knowledge about teachers different from using the traditional, direct question, "made up" interviews that most school administrators use.

The English Teacher: JoLynna

JoLynna is an experienced English teacher who Netzer had the opportunity to interview while trying to improve the teaching staff at Washington High School. Netzer recalls the interview with JoLynna. He had never seen a teacher quite like this; and, she had never experienced an interview quite like this. JoLynna was an experienced, successful teacher from a large urban district. She found it easy to get teaching jobs. She confidently stated that, "I could win the interview game with personality and wit." But when she ran into Dr. Netzer it was different. In reflecting on her interview, JoLynna's stated,

> In this interview I was wishing I had more deodorant. These questions were just relentless. It didn't let up, question after question. It felt like the longest hour of my life. As the questions continued it was coming clear to me that intellect and wit could not meet kids' needs. I had to be more than a good person to meet their needs and overcome the gaps they had in their achievement.
>
> During the interview my reflection was so inward, I could not make eye contact with him the whole time. Even though the scenarios in the questions were about fictitious students, I was seeing faces of students, real faces of real

students from my past teaching. The interview made me believe that he was going to expect me to be more, more of a teacher than I ever had been.

At the end of the interview, I had no idea how I had done. All I knew was that I had been incredibly honest. The only thing I knew was that I had to teach in a school that had a principal that asked questions like this.

The rest of this story is very interesting. JoLynna and her husband, also a teacher, had bought a house in the district near another high school in the district, the one at which they wanted to teach because everyone called it the "good high school." But, after a single interaction with Dr. Netzer and the experience of the Haberman STAR Teacher Interview, JoLynna said, "There was no question, we had to be at Washington High School." Dr. Netzer hired both JoLynna and her husband. They both still teach at Washington High School.

After the interview was over JoLynna said she had to unpack what she knew about teaching and think about how to "do it right." She reflected on "The Pedagogy of Poverty versus Good Teaching" (Haberman, 1991) where Haberman discussed how teachers and difficult students develop an unspoken agreement. The agreement has as its foundation, "If you leave me alone; I will leave you alone." Everyone just plays nice and expectations are unacceptably low. Students' lives are not changed. They leave school with few choices. JoLynna and others were hired because they knew this pedagogy of poverty had to change; all students deserved to be challenged, cared for and pushed to high expectations.

JoLynna is a teacher who loves to learn and is still growing; this is evident in her reflection on those first few years at Washington. "I have learned how to become a teacher. In the past I did things instinctually. Netzer helped me fashion it [teaching] into a craft. I am still mindful of that interview. It was not just about getting a job. I had to live up to my answers. He gave me the freedom to be the teacher I wanted to be. He believed I could be good."

TRANSFORMATION #2: VAN HORN HIGH SCHOOL

After five years at Washington High School, Netzer had the opportunity to do something that is rarely done in American education—the opportunity to re-open an urban high school. In 2008, Van Horn High School was one of the comprehensive high schools in the Kansas City, Missouri School District. Through state legislative action it was annexed to a nearby district and became the third high school in the Independence, Missouri School District. Similar to Washington High School, Van Horn served an impoverished community; different than Washington, the majority of the students at Van Horn were 65% White; 17% Hispanic; 13% Black and 3 % Asian. The school report card for Van Horn High School reads like any other diverse district in crises; low student performance and a climate that needed an overhaul by a leader committed to change.

In a local online newspaper interview, Netzer expressed the following about starting as the newly inducted school leader of Van Horn High School:

> I am impressed with the Independence School District's long-standing position in education community. This is basically like opening up a new school in many regards, which makes this new challenge exciting. I think there is a pressure to make sure we provide a quality education to the students of Van Horn High School. We want to guarantee that these kids are ready when they leave Van Horn as well as make sure we are building a community among the staff, students, parents, and members of the community. (Evenson, 2008)

With the "new opening" of Van Horn High School, Greg Netzer, as the new principal, had both the opportunity and the challenge of hiring the entire staff for a high school of approximately 750 students. Netzer's intent was to hire an entirely new staff using the Haberman STAR Teacher Interview. The process was lengthy. Netzer was consistently pushed by his new district to make decisions quickly, yet he was unwilling to settle for candidates who did not do well on the interview; he knew there were better ones out there.

Figure 1.1 Photo of Dr. Greg Netzer at Van Horn High School, 2008. *Source:* Julie Scheidegger—*The Examiner.* Reproduced with permission.

Greg is white.

The first year at Van Horn was difficult. Students were used to the impoverished teacher practices of yesteryear and Netzer had a new school culture he was charged with developing. Knowing that he had a school full of teachers who were committed to urban education and teaching students in poverty, Netzer set about to change the "pedagogy of poverty" typically practiced in urban high schools in America. He set about to create an urban high school with high levels of rigor, care, and expectation.

In addition to using the Haberman Star Teacher Selection Interview, Netzer utilized other practices touted by Haberman and germane to Netzer's beliefs about education. He fed his teachers a diet rich in reading that dealt with current educational innovations. He provided the opportunity for conversation, and he listened intently to what the teachers were saying. Highlighted as a building wide initiative, all classrooms began engaging in weekly Socratic Seminars. Initially, Netzer selected the text that everyone would use. Five years later, a group of teachers and students select the texts each week. As a result, students at Van Horn routinely engage in Socratic Seminars. Netzer believes this has had an impact on what students are heard saying and on the way they talk in classrooms throughout the school.

In 2013, five years after Netzer became principal at Van Horn, test scores and attendance rates have dramatically improved. In 2012, the student population was 66% White, 14% Black and 20% Hispanic. Seventy-seven percent of the students were on free and reduced lunch. 2012 data show that 65% of the graduates enter post-secondary education. English 1 and English 2 proficiency rates are 36% and 59%, respectively while algebra 1 and algebra 2 proficiency rates are at 35% each (Missouri Department of Elementary and Secondary Education, 2013).

Netzer attributes this success to the selection of his teachers; he believes the quality of the teachers allowed him to lead them through the reforms mentioned above. He modestly attributes the successes of the school to his teachers and his students. Conversely, his teachers attribute the success to Greg and the Haberman interview.

If you were to visit with teachers at Van Horn, you would consistently hear how the STAR teacher interview impacted them as a teacher new to the school. Netzer shares,

> Teachers felt that the new interview was fair, consistent, and a little daunting. When I informed them that their responses would be scored they were surprised. When candidates were offered positions most felt a sense of accomplishment. I tried to make it clear during the entire progression that the impact of teachers on student learning was the single most important internal factor on academic achievement and that this interview was created, in part, to identify teachers who possessed the skills to make a difference in a young person's life. This was a powerful message to send to applicants.

It is my opinion that the Haberman interview went a long way in helping to establish a professional culture. Teachers hired knew they were special. They felt professional. They knew they could make a difference. The interview instrument allowed me to make a decision based on science and not how I felt about a particular candidate. What a relief for me, and more importantly for the students in our school.

The Assistant Principal: Kristin

While we visited with Kristin, who is now the assistant principal and soon to be a new principal at one of Van Horn's feeder middle schools, it was clear the interview experience drew her to the school and working with this principal. Kristin states,

> This interview was the toughest experience ever. In one way it was fun and it made me think, and then think some more. The interview forced me to think about my practice and start to change. I would love to see his notes that he took when he interviewed me. It was the first time that I had ever been required to be that reflective, not even in graduate school. By the end of the interview I was saying to myself that I have to go to Van Horn.

> I didn't know if I was being successful during the interview. I knew I was being honest. Five years later I still remember who I talked about when he asked me that "love" question. Dr. Netzer does his evaluations of teachers the same way he does the interview. He asks what else I could have done to improve my lesson and after I give him one possibility, he asks for more.

The PE Teacher: Julie

Often teachers considered most critical to students' academic success are those who teach the core subjects of language art, math, science and social studies. However, the opportunity to visit with a Physical Education and Health teacher brought another perspective. This conversation illuminated the fact that, at Van Horn, teachers in all areas of a school build the environment to better serve all students. Julie became the P.E. and Health teacher the year of Van Horn's re-opening. Her reflections on her interview are surprisingly similar to reflections cited previously.

> I heard it was going to be a tough interview because of the constant digging for another answer. It immediately forced me to start looking at my classroom and what I needed to change. I couldn't tell if I was giving right answers or not. When I finished the interview I called my mother and told her that "I either failed the interview, or I knocked it out of the park." I was energized by

this. I had taught at another district school for 15 years and knew the kinds of things in that interview told me what we needed to start doing for students.

The Science Teacher: Jenny

When Jenny, a science teacher, reflected on her interview, she also recalls that it greatly impacted the ways in which she thought about her work.

> I had been interviewing with lots of districts. This interview was different. It was harder. He kept asking all of these follow-up questions. I thought I had done horribly. There was no way that I could tell if I was giving the right answer. The questions keep the students in mind. Five years later I still remember question number two.

After the interview and getting hired, I started looking into the Haberman literature. It proved to me that we could work with this population. Now I don't want to go back and work in a school that serves affluent kids.

WHY THE STAR TEACHER INTERVIEW WORKS

Over the years, Netzer had numerous conversations with Dr. Martin Haberman. From these conversations it became clear that the teacher interview was so skillfully crafted that it had the critical ingredient needed to find teachers committed to working with, building relationships with, and never giving up on students who had been underserved by America's educational system for most of their lives.

Netzer's reflection on the Haberman Interview as compared to typical district efforts to improve themselves strengthens the idea of why selection is so important.

> Part of the original district initiative included changing the structure of school; i.e., small learning communities, block schedules, curricular themes, weekly professional development time, etc. Although these are important ideas, in and of themselves, they proved to be insufficient. Another idea brought to the forefront by the original initiative was to build relationships with students. Unfortunately, much of this work was done in a structural way. What we now believe is that in order to build relationships with tough kids you have to hire staff who are committed to that kind of work. We found it very difficult to try to provide professional development that causes educators to want to build relationships with urban youth. This past year we were able to hire two replacement administrators using Haberman's interview instruments. Once again, we knew right away when we had the right candidates and what a difference they made. Hiring staff that have a desire to work with urban high school kids is clearly a critical piece to our performance improvement.

Using the STAR Teacher Interview is the launching pad for solid school improvement. Schools are made up of people who work with younger people in preparing them for a productive adult life. Effective schools are led by principals who not only hire the right people, but do something with it once the right teachers are in place. Dr. Netzer finished his reflection on being a high school principal this way:

> Our road ahead is full of educational dilemmas. I attended ten (10) student funerals in four years as principal. Too many of our kids are still not completing high school. We still have much improvement to make on state assessments. We still must make instructional and curricular improvements that allow our students to engage the world upon graduation. But, we are thrilled with the improvements. What do we believe led to the difference in performance among our high schools? We think trusting relationships between teachers and students had an impact. We had kids who worked hard in preparation for the state assessments during our interventions with them because of the relationship they had with teachers. We had kids who were thrilled when they found they had passed the tests and devastated when they didn't. Four years ago we had neither.

Now walking down the halls or welcoming students outside the building I get lots of greetings, a far cry from that first year. Our kids feel better about themselves and our staff believes they can make a difference in their students' lives.

Dr. Greg Netzer is retiring from the role of high school principal 18 months after the passing of Martin Haberman. Clearly, Dr. Haberman had a life changing impact on Netzer's life. Likewise, Netzer had a life changing impact on many teachers who, in turn, impacted and will continue to impact a great number of students.

> Finally, our goal in the school reform business is to improve student performance. I prefer to think that the processes we use to improve achievement are the important pieces that are often neglected. Hiring the right people helps to establish a professional culture. Hiring the right people increases the likelihood of improved collaboration and professional responsibility. Hiring the right people increases the opportunity for them to work together to enhance performance. Hiring the right people increases the probability of improved relationships between student(s) and teacher. Hiring the right people is a process that will lead to improved student performance. These processes are all enhanced by the use of Martin Haberman's very important work.

Having the right teachers with our young people improves lives. Dr. Haberman was right, "Selection is more important than training."

CHAPTER QUESTIONS

This chapter shares the ways in which one principal, with a short timeline to hire teachers yet a rigorous commitment to the STAR Teacher interview, created the foundation for a school on a steep improvement trajectory. Now, five years into the work, the school has shown dramatic academic improvements, in some cases equaling and surpassing the academic success of the other two middle class high schools in the district.

1. In what ways is Netzer's story similar, or different, to your own?
2. What are the current hiring and teacher selection practices at your school? What is your interpretation of their effectiveness?
3. What is needed to develop more stories of transformative high schools serving students in poverty?
4. Identify at least three mid-range functions exhibited by Dr. Netzer; be specific and explain the beliefs and behaviors.
5. Explain how contemporary principal models (i.e., licensing organizations or theoretical models) compare and contrast with Haberman's mid-range beliefs.

REFERENCES

Evenson, K. (2008). A new principal figure: Netzer named head administrator for Van Horn. *The Examiner*. Retrieved from http://www.examiner.net/article/20080709/NEWS/307099795

Gursky, D. (1992). Professor predicts urban teachers' success. *Education Week*. Retrieved from http://www.edweek.org/ew/articles/1992/04/01/28urban.h11.html

Haberman, M. (1991). The pedagogy of poverty versus good teaching. *Phi Delta Kappan, 73*(4), 290–294.

Haberman, M. (2002). *Can teacher education close the achievement gap?* Symposium at the Annual Meeting of the American Educational Research Association, April 2, 2002, New Orleans, LA.

Haberman Educational Foundation, Inc. (1994). *Star teacher selection interview training manual*. Houston, TX: The Haberman Educational Foundation, Inc.

Haberman, M. (2005). *Star teachers: The ideology and best practice of effective teachers of diverse children and youth in poverty*. San Antonio, TX: The Haberman Educational Foundation.

Kansas State Department of Education (2013a). *School report card 2003–2004*. Retrieved from http://svapp15586.ksde.org/rcard/building.aspx?org_no=D0500&bldg_no=8350

Kansas State Department of Education (2013b). *School report card 2007–2008*. Retrieved from http://svapp15586.ksde.org/rcard/building.aspx?org_no=D0500&bldg_no=8350

Missouri Department of Elementary and Secondary Education (2013). *Missouri Comprehensive Data System School Report Card*. Retrieved from http://mcds. dese.mo.gov/guidedinquiry/School%20Report%20Card/School%20 Report%20Card.aspx

CHAPTER 2

NO PRINCIPAL LEFT BEHIND?

The Core Beliefs of Nine Urban Elementary Principals in a Midwest School District Implementing No Child Left Behind

Rodney E. Watson
Valerie Hill-Jackson

CHAPTER OBJECTIVES

The learner will

1. Critique the daily lived reality of No Child Left Behind as it is experienced by urban elementary principles; and
2. Identify which characteristics of elementary school principals' core beliefs influence their ability to withstand the changing landscape of educational reform.

Better Principals, Better Schools, pages 15–35
Copyright © 2016 by Information Age Publishing
All rights of reproduction in any form reserved.

PRECIS

There is enormous benefit to understanding the daily impact of national educational reform efforts on school leadership since principals around the country are on the front line of implementation for all school improvement initiatives. But national school reforms are like buses, if you wait around long enough a new one is sure to come along shortly. For example, No Child Left Behind (NCLB), which is a re-ratification of the Elementary and Secondary Education Act (ESEA) of 1965, was passed by Congress in late 2001 and signed into law by President George W. Bush in January of 2002. The reauthorization represented a major change in the way schools were held accountable. Today, NCLB is being eclipsed by the latest whim of educational reform schemes, including: Common Core Standards, Race to the Top, teacher quality, teacher tenure, and the like. NCLB, once thought to be a permanent fixture in our national educational landscape, is now undergoing a slow demise by way of new ESEA flexibility as many U.S. states are asking for reform pardons (USDOE, 2014).

The passage of NCLB was followed by a decade of concerted activity across the states to produce an array of high-stakes accountability systems during the mid- and late 1990s that gradually grinded toward full implementation (Hess, 2003). The goals of NCLB include significant accountability standards in all public schools based on the premise that all children will be proficient in reading and mathematics by 2014. Other provisions include highly qualified teachers in every student classroom, improving parent communications, and making all schools safe environments for students. Failure to comply with NCLB mandates, as indicated through adequate yearly progress, could result in an array of consequences. Such consequences include being placed on a "needs improvement" list, mandated requirements of tutoring and other supplemental academic services, providing students with options to transfer to other in-district schools, or a loss of federal funds. It is no wonder, as Winter and Morgenthal (2002) warn, that high-stakes reform environments may hinder the identification and recruitment of talented school leaders.

Therefore, it is an appropriate time to assess if, or how, principals might withstand such unstable state and federal mandates. The voices of those who are charged with unpredictable implementation are rarely sought to evaluate how well reforms are being accomplished. Some principals will develop competence and resilience for enduring high-stakes reform, while others will have huge sanctions leveraged against their schools. Why do some principals weather the storm of reform while many are left behind?

This chapter begins with a brief discussion on school leadership and the nature of accountability under the weight of fluid reform agendas. It is worth speculating the ways a principal's core beliefs might impact reforms which are carried out in urban districts. Next, we unveil four themes that emerged from listening to the stories of nine Midwest urban elementary principals as they describe their understanding of the phenomenon of NCLB. For each of these themes, we interpret their voices through the lens of Haberman's star principal ideology. A short reflection closes this chapter.

A PRINCIPAL'S CORE BELIEFS AND REFORM

In an era of increased educational accountability and high-stakes testing as measured by NCLB, school districts seek administrators and building principals who embrace best practices in leadership, which may increase student achievement. Current trends toward the development or replication of programs, curricula, or school-based initiatives often give little regard for disposition of the leaders who are the stewards of reform at the school level. More attention has been given to principals' practice as opposed to practice driven by ideology.

Haberman (2005) describes core beliefs as a statement of fundamental convictions, values, and the overall character of an individual, which establishes that individual's moral and ethical priorities, which is uncompromising and serves to guide all of his or her activities. For the purposes of this study, lived experiences are defined as core beliefs, motives, acts, events, and actions related to the phenomenon of NCLB. Although there is no universal definition of the phrase core beliefs, the characteristics of one's core beliefs differs from individual to individual, often based on one's morals, values, culture, and beliefs. Selecting principals with the core beliefs that drive individuals to ensure children and youth should come first, at all cost, and is paramount to the success of students as well as principals and teachers. Stars have little tolerance for haphazard reform. Consequently, stars will feel a great deal of stress when they recognize the discrepancy between the ideal for NCLB and the real. Haberman maintains that, "Urban school bureaucracy is not benign. It sets up serious obstacles to teaching and learning. The star principal is on a constant vigil to mitigate the impact of this intrusive chaos" (p. 50).

Haberman explains that so as individuals think, they do. In other words, who we are becomes manifested in our behaviors. Therefore, ideology and behaviors are inextricably linked and the connection between stars' ideology and behaviors are fused. Haberman surmised that star principals have dispositions that protect them from the shifting demands of educational reform efforts:

> The attributes of star principals, which make them effective against all odds and in spite of irrational pressures, are more than behaviors. They are behaviors undergirded by an ideology. The ideology and the behaviors are interwo-

ven; they are of a piece. The connection between what star principals do and how they think about what they do cannot be broken. (Haberman, 1999, p. x)

Therefore, the way in which these nine principals chose to implement NCLB, or any reform, may be connected to their ideologies or core beliefs about schooling.

THE LIVING REALITIES OF NINE ELEMENTARY PRINCIPALS IMPLEMENTING NCLB

This chapter honors the voices of the nine elementary principals who are held accountable, day after day, for increased student achievement through the use of top-down mandates, high-stakes tests, directives, or edicts, without any regard to their fundamental beliefs about education, school culture, and the challenges in urban education. This study focused on elementary principals in a Midwest City in Missouri with a population of 480,623 and it is the twenty-fourth largest metropolitan area in the United States with a greater metropolitan population of 1.8 million. The larger sample consisted of 68 elementary principals representing four urban school districts located in Midwest City who have 25 or fewer years of elementary principal experience. From the larger sample, nine urban elementary principals were identified to gain deep, rich descriptions using a smaller sample to accentuate the NCLB phenomenon. The Haberman Urban Principal Interview instrument was not used to identify the principals.

Their stories were collected from the fall of 2004 to the spring of 2005, ranged from two to five hours, and were held in the principals' offices. In addition, observations were carried out in each elementary school and ranged from one to three hours. The interviews and observations were followed up by sending each principal a copy of the in-depth interview transcript for the purpose of gathering feedback and ensuring validity. By examining the principals words one gains insight into their core beliefs. Four big ideas, or themes, emerged from the conversations with the nine urban principals: (a) lack of knowledge; (b) NCLB accountability; (c) instructional leadership; and (d) voice.

Lack of NCLB Knowledge

The first of the four themes that emerged from the interviews relates to the elementary principals' perceived lack of knowledge of NCLB. The authors define lack of knowledge as a general lack of understanding of the expectations, components, and premise behind the development of NCLB legislation, including issues of race/ethnicity, class, and gender. Common first responses or descriptive phrases about NCLB were "Lack of training," "It's an accountability system," "Poor communication surrounding implementation," "It's all about high expectation," "Comparisons to other school districts is not fair," "Inadequate planning," and "AYP."

Much of the success of district and school leaders in building high performance organizations (organizations that make significantly greater than expected contributions to student learning) depends on how well these leaders interact with the larger social and organizational context in which they operate. All of the principals were aware of the legislation in its most basic form, but they were unable to discuss specifics about the components of NCLB and its effect on schooling. Will, who has been a principal for over 15 years, explained:

> I believe in the concept or the premise upon which NCLB was written. So while I like the idea that there is a standard, I am still concerned about our national perspective in terms of having a uniform standard and I [am] concerned about the fact that, um, the Adequate Yearly Progress, um, in some instances, does not reflect on the fact that we are not playing with a level playing field because there are some students that enter schools at different places and those different places then have an impact on the school's ability to make sure that students make the necessary gains. The legislation is too confusing and unclear."

is unclear, difficult to implement.

Although Will believed in the concept of NCLB, he focused more on the inequity of uniform standards, resources, and the lack of clarity within NCLB legislation. In comparison, Alicia, Ben, and Cindy also focused on the lack of knowledge and training and the need for uniform standards and measurement. They explained:

> You don't have everything to make sure you are not leaving any child behind but... there's a lack of training, there's a lack of knowledge, there's um... it's hard to explain or define as far as what NCLB is. We know what it is supposed to do so to speak, but the avenues that we need to take to get there, I think those are the things that... I imagine we all have questions about it. (Alicia)

> We need to look at it and we need to review it. We need to implement it the right way, so they just—no one wants to take blame. I think that on the ground level or ideally that it's a good idea, but I think that the planning was put into it wasn't adequate. There are just too many questions surrounding what it really is or means. (Ben)

> I really don't understand the legislation beyond all kids have to be perfect by 2014. I think it's almost based on a judgment now instead of just presenting um, information. (Cindy)

Observations also supported the lack of specific knowledge about NCLB. While I was observing in schools, information about NCLB legislation, components, or resources was not easily observable. Information was not observable on the walls or in print in any of the offices or classroom I visited. When the principals were asked about how they communicate NCLB legislation to their students or larger school community, Yolanda and Angel replied:

> We really don't talk about NCLB with parents past the accountability piece of making adequate yearly progress from year to year. (Yolanda)

> At our school, we talk to our kids about getting ready for the MAP test. We have assemblies, pep rallies, and family night activities that encourage our, um, parents to help get our kids ready. (Angel)

The narrative statements showed a limited understanding of NCLB or how it relates to the accountability of Adequate Yearly Progress. Yolanda and Angel shared common practices of information sharing with parents about the importance of helping their kids "get ready for the MAP test" and the importance of meeting the expectation of each yearly benchmark set for achieving AYP. Anything past benchmark attainment and yearly test preparation was marginalized or not discussed with the larger school community. In contrast, Ben and Will discussed their district's practices of educating parents and the larger school community by stating:

> Our district talks about NCLB components in our Town Hall meetings, but usually it's brief and you know, normally focuses on, um, um, did we make AYP for the year. (Ben)

> In the past, I gave parents a flyer that was given to me from district office, but I think the language was difficult for parents to understand. (Will)

Once again, Will and Ben discussed the district's attempt to provide parents and the larger school community education and insight into NCLB legislation; however, such information was limited to AYP benchmark results. Moreover, due to the difficulty in understanding NCLB legislation, conversations with parents did not provide opportunity for question and answer periods to deepen parents' or the community's understanding of the phenomenon. Upon review of Risa's monthly school newsletters, the mention of NCLB was during the months of October and November. Risa wrote a letter to her parents requesting increased parent support, and her teachers prepared their students for the MAP test in the spring. In a newsletter sent home to parents, Risa wrote:

> The Spring MAP Test is fast approaching. Please come, as teachers will share MAP strategies that you can use at home. We are excited about this opportu-

[handwritten margin note, rotated: "you need a to gain a clear understanding to relay to parent. community. staff. etc."]

nity and believe it will provide valuable support to You—as you in turn continue to support your child. (Risa)

Upon careful review of school improvement plans, weekly and monthly school newsletters, website information surrounding the school mission, vision and building goals and initiatives, there were no documents that mentioned NCLB past Risa's letter to her school community. If there is a "lack of knowledge" for the teaching staff and principals, in general, it stems from "lack of support" from the top staff or school boards making the mandatory decisions for a government proclamation. If NCLB had been expecting success beyond compare, the information provided would have come from the top with the appropriate time line for delivery and specific details for school leaders. If principals are working daily to ensure student success, it is the role of the bureaucracy to provide the message expectations, with adequate time to get the knowledge base out to the principals who will, in the long run, be held accountable for student success.

Principals in this study also shared the belief that inadequate planning led to a general lack of knowledge prior to the implementation of NCLB. Although many principals felt the legislation provided for checks and balances, they also felt the legislation was a good idea, a good premise, and increased their focus on the needs of students. Ben, Cindy, and Risa cited a lack of training, resources, and planning as factors that impede NCLB's success and respect.

> I think that on the ground level or ideally that it's a good idea, but I think that the planning that was put into it wasn't adequate. I don't think the research put into it was adequate so the implementation, I think, has doomed it and so it seems like every time they try to make a correction to what they have done so far, they fall in the same trap. (Ben)

> I think the general idea is good or the general idea of it was maybe well intentioned, but it is almost based on a judgment and I don't think the creators thought about the repercussions of such legislation. (Cindy)

> I think the premise is good and I think it increases the focus on all students, however I think there are just so many unanswered questions surrounding its development and purpose. It's not fair to think all kids will be perfect or proficient because that goes against all we know about diversity and how kids are different. There are good parts, but the planning is off. (Risa)

It is clear in the passages above that the principals have done some personal reflection on the clarity and usefulness of NCLB. Collectively, they point to confusion, lack of district and school level discussions, and poor planning as major obstacles for clarity and coordinated implementation. Haberman would encourage us to ask, "Where's the superintendent's voice on matters of reform?" and, "Has the groundwork been laid on the district level so principals can do the best they can?" Of course, each principal should be a life-long learner dedicated to self-directed learning, but negligence by the superintendent leaves the district blameless when NCLB, or any reform, fails. But reforms are too big to leave to chance. Each building principal should receive the same clearly articulated vision and mission on the science and art of NCLB implementation. The district CEO must assemble executive teams, often made up of principals, to confirm that every principal is armed with the required information to properly execute NCLB. Anything less than a carefully orchestrated plan, from the superintendent's office, is tantamount to educational genocide.

Haberman (1999) elucidates that the most enduring and impermeable school practices are never approved by the stakeholders they serve; they are the uncontested school rituals or reforms that school leaders simply inherit (p. 81). Haberman proposes that there are two guiding ideological positions that principals unwittingly adopt when dealing with obligatory projects or reform. First, job-holder principals often do not notice the inconsistency between high standards and the inadequate conditions under which the underserved urban learners will surely be evaluated and penalized because they do not have the necessary resources to achieve AYP. These status quo principals will continue to tout NCLB reform efforts and place the blame of success on poorly equipped students, families, and their teachers.

Alternatively, star principals are critically astute and will quickly identify the disconnect between reform ideal and the pitfalls that often impede full implementation for underserved learners. Stars will become enraged and find ways to hold these rituals up to public scrutiny so that challenges and problems for change become transparent as they work solutions within the context of their schools. The stars' methods of resistance may range from benign neglect of learning about NCLB to ensuring parent communication and preparing learners for state tests. Stars understand,

> When we use the phrase "leave no child behind" just what do we mean? Are we including 15 million children and youth in poverty? Members of minority groups? Those with handicapping conditions? . . . No child left behind has no meaning for those who need it most. (Haberman, 2003, p. 9)

NCLB Accountability

The accountability movement originated in long-standing efforts to measure cognitive aptitude and ability (West & Peterson, 2003). It is premised on the notion that standardized tests can and do measure an important dimension of education quality. Accountability has played and continues to play a major role in understanding NCLB and its impact on schools. As principals seek to understand the accountability of NCLB, they report feeling an increased sense of high expectations in the form of central office mandates, new programs, curriculums, and teacher resistance.

> The first problem the principal faces with a new district initiative is countering the impact of naysayers on his or her staff who warn teachers not to waste their enthusiasm on a "here today, gone tomorrow" project. In effect, the principal must work hard and with a total commitment to counter negators, knowing full well they may be correct. (Haberman, 1999, p. 83)

Accountability factors of NCLB include significant accountability standards in all public schools based on the premise that all children will be proficient in reading and mathematics by year 2014. Other accountability provisions include having highly qualified teachers in every student class, improving parent communications, and making all schools safe environments for students. Failure to comply with NCLB mandates, as indicated through adequate yearly progress, could result in an array of consequences. Such consequences include being placed on a "needs improvement" list, mandated requirements of tutoring and other supplemental academic services, providing students with options to transfer to other in-district schools, or a loss of federal funds.

The principals in this study understood the accountability factor of NCLB more than any other factor within the legislation because of the impacts of such factors on the daily activities of elementary principals. Principals Cindy, Yolanda, and Risa share their beliefs about NCLB and its effect within their schools.

> I like the accountability piece of NCLB. I think it is important that we are making teachers, buildings, and communities an accountable part for our kids. But I also think that it sets unrealistic goals. I think that um, the general idea of it was maybe well intentioned, but it is almost based on a judgment now instead of just presenting, um, information. Um, lofty ideas. That's all. (Cindy)

> I know that there has to be accountability. I think there are some good things about making Adequate Yearly Progress. I don't have problems with accountability; I don't have problems with accountability for me. It's just how are we going to go about doing that and not . . . really not wanting to leave any child behind, but doing that. That's just my belief. (Yolanda)

> I think accountability is good. It increases our focus on students we have not been concerned with. I think it's great because it's raised the level of awareness of how we look at kids from different lenses. I think the frustration is that there are so many factors that impact our ability to make sure we reach our goals. (Risa)

School documents showed accountability as high in priority as well. School Improvement Plans showed evidence of reading and math goals as indicators of success and suggested increased student achievement in reading and mathematics as evident in Adequate Yearly Progress results as proof of accountability. Document and observational data illuminated such findings further.

> Our staff will reach state mandated average yearly progress goals by modifying, developing, and expanding curriculum, assessment, and instructional programs to address the diverse educational needs of our community. (Ben)

> We will create after-school programs that support the teaching and remediation of key skills, thus increasing student achievement in the areas of communication arts and math. (Angel)

> We will increase the number of students scoring in the top two categories (Communication Arts and Mathematics) on local and state assessments by 15%. (Yolanda)

> Staff will submit weekly lesson plans that show evidence of their knowledge of effective instructional practices that meet the learning styles of each child. (Alicia)

> Our staff will administer quarterly district common assessments in reading and math and develop strategies that support increased achievement. (Will)

Various types of accountability were evident throughout school improvement plan goal statements. As I reviewed various activities, outcomes, and indicators of success within the various building school improvement plans, several buildings increased their expectations in an effort to meet the accountability standard or goal of AYP.

One common descriptor among many of the elementary principals was the notion of high expectations. The elementary principals in this study were aware of the need for accountability and the need to have quality teachers in classrooms. However, they noted that it is essential to have high expectations for students and teachers as they seek to meet the yearly benchmarks set in AYP. Effective school research defined the role for the instructional leader as "high expectations for teachers and students, close supervision of classroom instruction, coordination of the school's curriculum, and close monitoring of student progress" (Hallinger, 1992, p. 37). As elementary principals discussed high expectations, Alicia, Angel, and Ben placed attention on the need to have high expectations for administrators, teachers, parents, and the community as they seek to meet AYP. Alicia, Angel, and Ben stated:

> It is our expectation that we all have a responsibility even if mom, dad, grandma . . . if they don't do their part, it is still our responsibility as a school community to do what we need to do for kids. (Alicia)

We have high expectations. We might have challenges here but the bottom line is you are their teacher and you are the secretary and you have a job to do. I do the walkthroughs, putting things down that reflect back what I see them doing which is going back to the things that we have been trained in. (Angel)

I think it's the role of the administrator and sometime it's the role of different teachers in the building and it's stepping up and being an example, showing teachers what they need to aspire to and giving them the help. It's also being a resource for them, being in the classroom and observing what they are doing by giving them positive feedback, and keeping up on the research. (Ben)

The tone in these principals' voices suggests that they assume ultimate responsibility for the educational outcomes of their school serving children in poverty.

Haberman (1999) explains that there are two extreme views for principals on the issue of educational accountability—star and status quo thinking. Status quo principals are likely to explain NCLB failure on the students' ability or their family and community conditions.

Blaming the victim, his or her family, and the community for lack of school success—and attributing school success to innate ability—predisposes the holders of these views to rationalize their inaction and lack of accountability. Those who hold such beliefs ask, "What can you expect the school (or me) to do about all the debilitating conditions of urban poverty? What can schools do with children who have less ability?" They explain the problems facing students at risk of failure by citing factors outside of the aegis of the school. Their reasoning is that, if the causes of at risk students exist in conditions outside the school, then the solutions must exist outside the school as well. (p. 37)

Haberman scorns, that when it comes to taking responsibility, many principals would rather point out a window, assigning blame to a child's environment as opposed to looking in a mirror. While stars understand the devastating effects of poverty on urban learners, they do not place the sole liability for underachievement on the backs of the learners or their families, but also hold the educational environment accountable. Stars,

also identify problems caused by schools—for example, poor teachers, inadequate curriculum, overcrowded classrooms, or inadequate materials and equipment—that might place youngsters at risk of failing or dropping out.... They maintain that the school has the power to engage students in meaningful learning regardless, or in spite of, living conditions. (p. 37)

Stars understand that the lofty task of meeting AYP is not simple but remain committed to modeling a positive philosophy among the stakeholders that their collective efforts can help students become successful.

Instructional Leadership

The third of the four themes that surfaced from the interviews relates to the role of the elementary principal as instructional leader. Lambert (2002) suggests that the days of the principal as the lone instructional leader are over because no one administrator can serve as the instructional leader for an entire school without the substantial participation of other educators. ." Such a feeling was manifested in the descriptive codes of teacher-leadership and collaboration among school stakeholders that later led to the development of the theme or category of instructional leadership. Therefore, the old model of formal, one-person leadership leaves the substantial talents of teachers largely untapped. Although instructional leadership is a term that is widely used, its definition among educational leaders seem somewhat vague. For the purposes of this study, instructional leadership refers to possessing or demonstrating characteristics of direct assistance to teachers, group development, staff development, curriculum development, and action research, which all serve as precursors to the theme or category of instructional leadership.

Current research confirms that students achieve more in schools whose principals are seen as strong leaders. Effective schools must have effective leaders who can create and implement a vision of the school's culture that contains within it the values on which excellence is built. Throughout the in-depth interviews, many of the elementary principals shared their feelings about the concepts of instructional leadership. Several comments centered on instructional leadership being "a vehicle for every principal," "placing instruction first," "collaborating with staff," and "a role of every teacher in the building.

The elementary principals through the following narrative statements illuminated the role of instructional leadership.

> Instructional leadership encompasses a lot. It's a vehicle of every principal. My definition that I wrote for myself was the ability to create an atmosphere where effective teaching and student success is at the heart of every decision that the staff members make. I think it's important that classroom teachers are seen as instructional leaders, that, uh, secretaries are seen as instructional leaders in the office, the cafeteria, um, that everybody sees themselves as a leader in their specific roles. (Cindy)

> Instructional leadership is being a teacher leader, having or placing instruction first and foremost from student achievement and not from what teachers are doing. Being the instructional leader means, you know, dissecting that and putting it out on the table for collaborations for discussion with staff members to look at how are the patterns that we see, you know, going to transcend then into what our building goals are going to be instructionally. Its making sure that people have input at all levels but that we also give them good information so

that we are knowledgeable in our input. It's making sure that you have some structures in place so that there is a consistent review of data, building initiatives, instructional initiative of what are all working on and accountability, you know, looking into classrooms and giving feedback. (Risa)

Instructional leadership is the role of the administrator and sometimes it's the role of, of different teachers that are in the building and it's stepping up and being an example, um showing teachers what they need to, to aspire to and giving them the help or facilitating them with the resources they need. It's being out in the middle of things all of the time. (Ben)

Instructional leadership is creating basically a climate where you're helping to create a climate where your staff . . . everyone in your staff takes responsibility. Your entire staff takes responsibility to make sure that the kids are achieving academically. It's making sure that those best practices are implemented so the kids can achieve. (Alicia)

Instructional leadership is being that person who knows the latest, the trends, and best practices and being able to model that and give that to teachers. It's providing teachers with those resources and those things that we need to get the job done as an instructional leader. It means you know instruction, curriculum and you know management needed to run a school. (Angel)

It was obvious through the aforementioned narratives that the core beliefs around issues of instructional leadership for these elementary principals rested on the beliefs of shared decision-making, collaboration, teacher leadership, responsibility, and elementary principal knowledge of curriculum, data, and school culture. Haberman (1999) maintains that,

To function as the instructional leader, the principal must know and keep current with the most effective methods of instruction for generating results with students. He or she must be an expert consumer of these instructional strategies in order to answer two questions: How can teachers learn, practice, and improve effective strategies? What conditions can he or she provide to facilitating these activities? (p. 46)

Haberman also insinuates,

To function as a genuine instructional leader of the school and not its business manager, the principal must demonstrate certain attributes. Foremost is the willingness to be accountable. The principal who says, "The university prepared these teachers and the Human Resources Department hired them, so what do you want from me?" does not understand the accountability model under which he or she is operating. (p. 44)

Observations also supported the theme of accountable instructional leadership. While in various school settings, I observed Alexandria who discussed the importance of following the district curriculum guide and implementing balanced literacy with depth and passion. I also observed Will and Risa walking around the building conducting walkthroughs in individual classrooms based on specific look-fors that they reported being developed through a collaborative process with building teachers. In addition, Ben attended a grade level meeting at which he listened to first grade teachers discuss their students' reading progress as they charted individual student reading progress.

Haberman (1999) reminds us that stars value the knowledge and wisdom of parents and caregivers in the community and believe they want the best for their children. Whether the principal regards parents and caregivers as people of worth and as parents in the educational mission manifests in the way he or she speaks, stands, sits, greets and interacts with them (p. 88). Instances of such behavior demonstrating such courtesy were evident in the principals' copies of individual building mission statements, school improvement plans, and monthly newsletters supported the theme of instructional leadership through the following written statements:

> Our school envisions a basic school climate filled with students, teachers, and parents who embrace rigorous instruction and high expectations that are aligned to Missouri's State Standards. Our diverse community will use Balanced Literacy, Essential Elements of Instruction, service learning and technology to create an educational community that enriches us all. (Alexandria)

> Mark your calendars for February 15, when our school will host our 5th grade students' Living Museum and our Math Night. You will have an opportunity to go through interactive math stations where your child can earn money to spend at the math store at the end of the event. (Yolanda)

> Your hard work is paying off and we thank you for your help in working with your child on QAR, Reading Comprehension Strategies, the Super 7 Math Problems-Solving strategies, and mastering their grade level communication arts and mathematics academic benchmarks. We are seeing that students are having more success as they participate in higher-order thinking tasks that are occurring in the classroom. (Risa)

Throughout the study, each elementary principal also discussed the role that teacher accountability plays within his or her definition or understanding of accountability within the elementary principalship. In doing so, Angel, Alicia, and Yolanda illuminated the need for "conversations," "being specific," "responsibility," and "close supervision."

> I have those conversations with teachers or staff members, whatever the situation would be, and follow up and that's how accountability comes into play. Not just checking up or just asking, but being real specific in the type of questions that you ask so they know what's important. (Angel)

I believe it's my responsibility; it's my duty to make sure that we all take responsibility for each other so that the supervision is there. It's my job to make sure that we come up with a system of accountability where we are all accountable for the success of our kids and supervising that. Supervision, it's an accountability piece. It's a system of accountability. (Alicia)

Accountability is important. It requires a lot of supervision, monitoring, and assisting to see what strategies or what techniques, what methodologies are you using today. (Yolanda)

Teacher accountability played a critical role in this study. Haberman proposes (1999),

The essential job of the principal in implementing a belief in students' potential is to move teachers from blaming the victim to assuming accountability for what and how much children can learn. For principals to accomplish this task, he or she must personally believe in students' potential. (p. 38)

(Stars defy a pedagogy of poverty in which students are managed and teachers are tracked for compliance.) Instead, generating student engagement and motivation are seen as the primary functions of teaching. "Whenever teachers can make a learning activity of intrinsic value, it is possible to transform children into genuine learners" (Haberman, 1999, p. 24).

Field observations illuminated important information on how teacher accountability was infused throughout the course of the school day.

At the beginning of the day, we walked around the entire building to say hello to all of the staff. While walking around, we looked at each teacher's desk to make sure his or her lesson plan book was available and complete. (Will) —Collab

Today, we sat in a grade-level meeting with four first-grade teachers. Throughout the meeting the teachers discuss theme units, calendar activities, and balanced literacy strategies. Mrs. Alexandria sat in the meeting for about an hour and participated in the discussion around literacy. Mrs. Alexandria asked questions and discuss what skills needed to be taught according to the curriculum guide. (Alexandria) collab

I [first author] walked around the building with Risa. It is evident that she is in classrooms often. All of the kids know her and seem to look forward to her visits. In several of the classrooms, she knew what activity or lesson was being taught, because some of the kids were asking her to help them finish what they started the previous day. (Risa)

I [first author] sat in a staff meeting with Angel as she discussed Bloom's Taxonomy. Angel provided data to support the need to teach at deeper levels. Angel reviewed the previous week's staff development and provided an opportunity for teachers to show their peers examples of how they implemented

Bloom's and provided a mini-lesson as an example to help teachers understand what's expected within their classroom. (Angel)

It was evident that several of the elementary principals understood that it would take more than their individual talents, gifts, and insights to truly improve their school. Their success rested in the collective inquiry of other school stakeholders. The following narrative statements support such findings.

I believe in working with people in a positive manner, making sure that we have collaborative relationships among all of the adults in our school, making sure that people that come into our school feel welcome and have a voice. I believe in making sure that we move by consensus. (Will)

I'm always interested in the conversation. We sit down and talk. If there's a problem we work collaboratively to solve the issue. Because we work collaboratively and because they have to come back together having done the work they said they were going to do in the classroom we all are accountable to each other. (Alexandria)

Everything we do is for the kids. That is how we are going to make our decisions. I think it is hard for the principal, but I think that is crucial that we do that and that we keep reminding people what we are here for. I mean you've got to think be a great team building, have good rapport, be collaborative. In order to get things done you have to have relationship with people. We work really hard on us and getting ourselves together and getting those relationships build and getting those priorities set and the vision in getting the parents in as you know, stakeholders and, you know, we work hard on being approachable. (Risa)

We collaborate in looking where we are, where we are as a school, by looking at our data, working with the staff, and looking at it and working with the data to see . . . to make informed decisions to see where we are, where do we need to go. We believe strongly in collaboration and sometimes I think maybe, I collaborate a little too much. Sometimes, teachers say just tell me what you want me to do. You know, it's my duty to make sure that we all . . . that we do take responsibility for each other. (Alicia)

You know, we have those conversations with teachers or staff members, whatever the situation would be and following we follow up by looking at our building goals to see if we met our goals for math and what we said was our benchmark. (Angel)

If you walked around with me, you would see teachers collaborating together during their plan time. We are very supportive of each other because it takes all of us to make this happen. (Cindy)

Collaboration was a common descriptor that illuminated through documents, as well as field observations. While capturing and bringing to light the stories of elementary principals as they attempted to understand the phenomenon of NCLB, documents and observation field notes provided further illumination. In addition, various school written mission statements served to confirm the principals' commitment to achievement:

> We will maximize parents' and community efforts to improve student performance. Together, we can make a difference. (Yolanda)

> It is our mission to serve the whole child through the four priorities of the Basic School Philosophy. The four priorities are: School as Community, Curriculum with Coherence, Climate for Learning, and Commitment to Character. (Will)

> Our school is supported by active and committed parents who strive to work collaboratively with the school to achieve the goals and mission for our children. (Angel)

> Community partnerships are essential at our school. We have a large Hispanic population and without us sitting down with parents and working together to plan and develop supports for um, our students, we would not be able to do this in isolation. Collaboration is key. (Alexandria)

Haberman advises that the school and local communities must come together in cooperative ways in order to reach educational objectives, and "the notion that the principal can function as an independent decision maker is dangerous. The more important an issue, the greater the likelihood that the principal will need additional information and wider consultation with others" (p. 67).

Voice

The fourth theme that emerged from the data related to the elementary principals was voice regarding the phenomenon of NCLB. Voice, for the purpose of this study, is defined as an individual's ability to articulate and describe their wants, needs, desires, interpretations, and beliefs about issues that directly affect their role/function and society's expectation of school leadership. Paramount to the development of the theme or category of voice were the descriptors: "being supportive," "serving the people," "living by example," "listening," "effective communication," "relationships," and "raising difficult issues around race, class, and gender," "questioning." [Throughout my study, many of the elementary principals felt their voice was silenced because no one ever asked them what they needed as they attempted to meet the accountabilities of NCLB] Although several of the elementary principals were able to clearly define their role in relation to instructional leadership, such definitions were also manifested in schools as field observations were conducted. Nevertheless, a lack of reciprocity was evident between the voice the elementary principal attempted to create among teachers and other school stakeholders in comparison to voice between the elementary principal and their immediate supervisor. An understanding of this lack of reciprocity was illuminated in the narrative statements of several elementary principals.

> I really don't feel like my voice is heard. Nobody asked, to my knowledge about our feelings about new programs or initiatives that we are supposed to support in our buildings. I feel disrespected in the sense that they don't care. Nobody asks you anything quite frankly. Um, you go, you go to principal meeting and you hear all this stuff coming down. You know you walk in feeling good and you walk out going "Oh Lord" and then you go back to your building and you get back into rhythm and things are fine. (Alexandria)

> I feel I am listened to when I have a question. However, I am not asked what I need from central office. What do you need is a different question than, what are you doing? I am very seldom asked anything. (Alicia)

> I am heard at principal meeting if I have a question. No one ever asks what I need. Usually only the people who complain get heard. I may say something, but I usually go back and resolve it or I'll fix it or I'll make it work so nothing really happens. (Yolanda)

> I never get formal requests for opinions. It seems like a pie in the sky thing. You just get mandates and told what you are supposed to do for the year and it goes in your school improvement plan. (Cindy)

> I don't have a voice. Well I have a voice, but I think I am being blown off. We never get asked what we need; we only get told what the next agenda item is for the year. I tend to speak out more on some things when I probably should shut up, but I think that makes a difference and I have been here for a while. (Ben)

Although many of the elementary principals felt their voices were diminished or silenced, such diminishments only related to conditions about their lived experiences with their immediate supervisor or district office personnel. No one was listening to the principals and they should not be left on an island to fend for themselves. While conversations with colleagues can be very important, consistent interaction between the central office staff while making plans for any future activities that are required to bring improvements. The superintendent's office must be open to hearing suggestions from those who may be experiencing problems within the organization. Every successful principal generally invites and offers suggestions; suggestions that can and will be addressed for the betterment of the workplace and in the classroom. Building effective schools requires that every principal has an opportunity to share ideas upward and given the feedback and engaged dialogue that supports school improvement. Superintendents and principals should be able to say, "We are all in this together"!

In previous themes within this chapter, elementary principals were able to clearly differentiate and link individuals and systems to their fundamental beliefs about instructional leadership and collaboration within their school, which clearly illuminated their voice within their natural setting. However, the elementary principal's voice that resonated through school improvement plans and newsletters was in actuality the voice of district office or the elementary principal's immediate supervisor in an attempt to meet the expectations of district Comprehensive School Improvement Plan (CSIP) goals and NCLB.

UPON REFLECTION

While the jury is still out on whether or not the nine principals presented in this chapter are stars, it is helpful to look at the lived realities of everyday principals who endure contested and often short-lived reform for which they are held accountable. The consequences of understanding principals' core beliefs, star or status quo, become magnified under the pressures of NCLB or any fleeting reform agenda since implementation is at the center of the principal's role. The implications of principals' core beliefs and reform implementation are too expansive to tackle here, but must be taken up in future research.

Four big ideas, or themes, emerged from the conversations with the nine urban principals: (a) lack of knowledge; (b) NCLB accountability; (c) instructional leadership; and (d) voice. Upon reflection, Haberman surely would have identified the interesting paradox of these themes drawn from the nine principals who appear to be surviving NCLB. The interviews and observations demonstrate that their ideologies on schooling impact how they implemented NCLB. The principals in this study admit to a lack of knowledge and voice in matters related to NCLB, yet these well-intentioned principals work hard to meet all school level accountability mandates and requirements while giving the stakeholders in their schools the instructional leadership they deserve. These nine principals acknowledge uncoordinated plans and information on the district level, but do not allow such ambiguity to interfere with supporting their stakeholders on the school level. Stars carefully navigate this terrain in a way to protect their schools, while meeting the nonsensical expectations of district, state or federal mandates. While a lack of knowledge about NCLB and voice may be indicators of an ill-informed and disregarded leader, the star principal is quite clear and understands what she or he can actually control. This type of dogged, resolute focus serves as a type of immunization from the irrational malady of educational reform.

Therefore, when stars attempt to make positive changes within their schools they will do so in a vacuum with the perception that their voices, beyond the school, do not matter. Effective principals have to reconcile the outside (district level challenges of reform) with the inside (school related matters that support stakeholders). Star principals persist in their unrelenting attention on the students, and find ways to settle the inconsistencies by meeting the needs of underserved learners in our ever-changing age of accountability.

Star principals always weather the storms of reform by placing children in poverty first. The noise of reform does not interfere with protecting the schools of stars because of their singular commitment to children and justice.

CHAPTER QUESTIONS

1. Compare and contrast the comments made by the nine principals under the theme of "lack of knowledge." Who, if anyone, exemplifies the sentiments of a star principal and explain the rationale for your answer.
2. Identify two principals in this study and explain the relationship between the way they implemented NCLB and their core beliefs on schooling.
3. How are today's school leaders affected by the changing landscape of reform? What strategies have you used to combat reform fatigue?
4. What new reform agenda do you foresee as a challenge for urban school principals? Explain your choice.
5. The Haberman Urban Principal Interview instrument was not used to identify principals for this study. Does it matter if the study participants were stars? Why or why not?
6. As a building or district leader, how might you go about creating an action plan for implementation? In your response, be sure to include all of the stakeholders you feel may be affected by your proposal.
7. What are the implications of hiring status quo principals when new reform is being implemented?
8. The Common Core is currently under adoption by most states across the United States. What are the standards or provisions for administrators or principals and how do these Common Core standards stack up to Haberman's 11 core functions?

REFERENCES

Haberman, M. (1999). *Star principals serving children in poverty.* Indianapolis, IN: Kappa Delta Pi.

Haberman, M. (2003, Fall). No Child Left Behind: A promise made is a debt unpaid. Who will deliver? *The Haberman Newsletter, 8*(1). Retrieved from http://www.altcert.org/Documents/fall_2003.pdf

Haberman, M. (2005). Star teachers: *The ideology and best practices of effective teachers of diverse children and youth in poverty.* Houston, TX: The Haberman Educational Foundation.

Hallinger, P. (1992). The evolving role of American principals: From managerial to instructional to transformational leaders. *Journal of Educational Administration, 30*(3), 35–48.

Hess, F. M. (2003). Refining or retreating? High-stakes accountability in the states. In Peterson, P. E. & West, M. R. (Eds.), *No child left behind: The politics and practice of school accountability* (pp. 55–74). Washington, DC: Brookings Institution.

Lambert, L. (2002). A framework for shared leadership. *Educational Leadership, 59*(8), 37–40.

No Child Left Behind (NCLB) Act of 2001, Pub. L. No. 107-110, § 6319, Stat 20 (2008).

United States Department of Education (USDOE). (2014). *ESEA flexibility.* Retrieved from http://www2.ed.gov/policy/elsec/guid/esea-flexibility/index.html

West, M., & Peterson, P. (2003). *No child left behind: The politics and practice of school accountability.* Washington, DC: Brookings Institution Press.

Winter, P. A., & Morgenthal, J. R. (2002). Principal recruitment in a reform environment: Effects of school achievement and school level on applicant attraction to the job. *Educational Administration Quarterly, 38*(3), 319–240.

1. @ 1st glance, NCLB seems like a great foundational leg. for schools to excel and keep track of it.

2.

3.

4. B/c principals didn't recieve the support they needed to

5. Effective prinapals must always remember the needs of the students, families and communities and center any other huddle (such as the confusion from NCLB) as one that must prioritize "the orginal pean."

5 Key points!

? : How do principals understand and help their teachers implement common core standards?

properly and successfully implement NCLB, principals ran into issues revolving around: lack of understanding, defining leadership roles, etc.

CHAPTER 3

THE OTHER SIDE
OF THE DESK

The Beliefs and Behaviors
of Star Principals at Turnaround Schools

Jim Robins

CHAPTER OBJECTIVES

The learner will

1. Explore a case study of star principals selected with The Haberman Pre-Screener tool and interview;
2. Understand what star principals know, do, and believe in turnaround schools, and;
3. Analyze the impact that star principals make on student achievement and teachers.

Recently, I completed a research project that attempted to determine what beliefs and attitudes were commonly held by principals in the greater Kansas City area. I wanted to know how teachers were selected and how these

Better Principals, Better Schools, pages 37–47
Copyright © 2016 by Information Age Publishing
All rights of reproduction in any form reserved.

beliefs and attitudes guided principals within this process. My prior research indicated that there was a gaping hole in our knowledge of the work of Dr. Martin Haberman; most of what is written on his scholarship emphasizes the impact on student achievement in urban settings. In addition, many of us are already familiar with Haberman's research on interviewing and selecting teachers and principals. So, while we have documented studies on outcomes and selection, a chasm still exists in the literature for understanding what star principals know, believe, and do in their professional environments.

My study led me to talk with many principals in our area and this investigation gave me a much better understanding of how effective star principals operate within the context of their schools. I was interested in learning more about the beliefs and behaviors of principals, not from the perspective of students, but from the "other side of the [principal's] desk." What could we learn about the attitudes and beliefs of principals who were selected with the Haberman Pre-Screener and Interview protocol? What could we learn about the attitudes and beliefs of star principals who use the Haberman system in selecting teachers? Would there be common attitudes and beliefs that could be a driving force in the work of successful principals?

With this in mind, I decided to interview 20 Kansas City area principals who had been identified with the Pre-Screener and *The Haberman Star Administrator Selection Interview* and trained in the art of selecting teachers. The development of this questionnaire involved merging the knowledge and research base with the most effective practices of star urban principals. The research and theory base were summarized in the 24 domains of the Knowledge and Skill Base and laid out in *Principals for Our Changing Schools* published by The National Policy Board for Educational Administration (Haberman, 2003, p. 1). The Haberman Administrator Pre-Screener tool was developed after decades exploring principals' successes and failures— primarily focused on urban school districts. He performed exit interviews with principals who were retiring from the profession. Haberman's research revealed the beliefs and behaviors that administrators should possess when leading school improvement among underserved learners; especially those children who come from diverse backgrounds burdened by urban poverty. From this research, Haberman developed key dispositions that principals in urban settings must possess in order to be successful. These dispositions include the following foci:

- An uncompromising passion for leading in schools where there are populations of at-risk students;
- A positive learning environment through creative problem solving and persistence that will find the optimal solution to tackle challenges that children encounter;

- The creation of a collaborative and encouraging school culture that supports teaching and learning for children and adults, and;
- An appreciation of parent, caretaker, and community knowledge and a reverence for their role as essential stakeholders and partners in the education process. (Haberman, 1999; 2004)

The interviews I conducted with the 20 principals were designed to allow stars to talk (and for me to listen) so that these attitudes and beliefs could emerge from their remarks. The quantitative data from the survey showed a clear and consistent pattern of thinking and behavior. The qualitative data, found in the hours of interviews I compiled, showed a group of principals who truly believed in the Haberman system and who believed very strongly in the importance of the work that they were doing. Each star principal in my study was asked to prioritize Haberman's 11 core functions, and the results of my study were very clear. Almost every star principal, of Haberman's 11 core functions (see Chapter 5), demonstrated:

1. The ability to show persistence in leading underserved learners and;
2. The understanding of the nature of at-risk children and the ability to work with them were of paramount importance.

Now, this was more than lofty speculation as each of these star principals was a leader in a successful school with underserved learners; indeed, they were walking the talk! They were more than principals, but star principals who leveraged their Haberman training to also select star teachers to turn around their schools.

I then selected two of the principals to participate in additional interviews in order to gain a more intimate perspective on what star principals know, believe, and do. The first star principal, Mr. Clem Ukoama, is a high school principal in a charter school in inner city Kansas City. Second, I will share a profile on Christy Compton who is a principal in an elementary school in Independence, Missouri. Both of these stars possess stellar leadership abilities and an unwavering commitment to at-risk youth. This chapter is organized around Clem and Christie's experiences as Haberman trained principals who have interesting perspectives from "the other side of the desk."

PRINCIPAL CLEM

"Student Failure Just Makes Me Crazy"

Clem Ukoama is a high school principal at University Academy in Kansas City, Missouri. His school is ranked as one of the top two academic high schools in the Kansas City area on the basis of the testing program of the state of Missouri. Clem's student body is over 90% African American and the percentage of students at University Academy who are eligible for free-lunch programs is over 70%. Students at this school are expected to attend college and are exposed to a rigorous college preparatory curriculum. Last year's 37 graduates received over 2 million dollars in college scholarship money. A large board in the foyer of the school displays a map of the various colleges around the United States that have University Academy graduates as current students. University Academy is "the charter school" to attend in the Kansas City area and is known for academic excellence.

Clem is a visible presence in the high school. His booming voice and powerful personality resonate within the school as he interacts with students and staff. As you talk with Clem, you realize that his background as a native of Nigeria allows him to share a unique style and perspective with the students and staff of University Academy. As he talks about his school and the problems that he faces each day you realize that this is a man who doesn't fear the future. Years of success with students at University Academy have allowed Clem to refine his beliefs and practices in a real world setting. Clem shared that the Haberman system had "been useful to me as an administrator in helping me to understand that urban teaching is totally different form rural teaching." For Clem, he sees the students who walk the halls of University Academy as promising young men and women. His philosophy of leadership is encapsulated in his remark to me that "it is the failure of students that drives me crazy."

Clem's journey to becoming a school leader was far from a straight line. Educated and raised in the African nation of Nigeria, Clem came to the United States with the intention of pursuing a career in business. After earning an MBA and spending several years in retail business, Clem was encouraged by friends to try teaching. Now almost a quarter of a century later, he brings a unique perspective to his work and to the challenge of a leader at an urban school with high expectations. Almost 25 years of school leadership have led him to believe that providing a structure for students to be successful is crucial to having a great school.

High Expectations and Effort for Urban Learners

Clem shares the case of one of his students as an example of what my research refers to as persistence. He opened up to me with the story of a young man (whom we will refer to as DC) who would not apply himself; DC just refused to spend the time to study in order to pass his freshman algebra class. DC was capable of much more yet was willing to fail rather than make the extra effort to raise his grade. In the typical school setting, DC would

student environment correlates
to student success.
The Other Side of the Desk ▪ **41**

move on to his sophomore year knowing that at some point he either needs to retake algebra to get his needed math credit or take a lesser math course.

Luckily for DC, he was not a student in a school with a typical principal. I find in the behavior of Mr. Clem Ukoama the same quality that was evident in my research project on successful principals. Behind Clem's assertion that "student failure just makes me crazy" was a dogged persistence that will not allow the star principal (or the star teacher) to accept failure as an option. Again and again in my interviews of principals, I heard the same common refrain that teacher persistence (and principal persistence) demands the attitude of "never give up" on students or on high expectations.

For DC, this meant that algebra was now a class that he took twice each day. Gone was his favorite class, the one in which he did weight training to prepare for his anticipated future career in sports. Under Mr. Ukoama's plan, DC would attend his algebra class each morning and take the same class again in the afternoon with a special tutor assigned to him for the second session. Additional time after school was allotted if necessary to drive home the point that algebra would be mastered regardless of the difficulty or the time necessary to achieve success. The student would persevere until he was successful in algebra. *how is this even possible?*

Success as a key component of the high school structure was tied to mastery learning in Mr. Ukoma's eyes. During his time at University Academy, the curriculum was redesigned to compel students to achieve mastery of key concepts at an 80% or better level before moving on to the next concept. The emphasis on expertise and the accelerated college preparatory curriculum have created an environment in which inner city children have been able to compete successfully with suburban schools in the Kansas City Area. In fact, a recent listing of Kansas City area schools on Missouri's Annual Performance Report showed University Academy as one of the top schools in the area and in the state. *is mastery of a content the only goal? priority*

Clem tells me that he studies his failures far more than his successes. For the star principal, the mark of success is not the top student's progress but the ability of that principal to structure a school environment that compels all students to succeed. DC had already failed a grade in middle school prior to coming to high school. He had a 25% grade in algebra when Mr. Ukoama put the new plan in motion. Mr. Ukoama's study of this failure had produced a clear plan of action.

Haberman explains that star principals consistently fight the ideology of unemployment with teachers and students with an ideology of mastery. Curricula in ineffective schools resists knowledge that scaffolds, but requires learning enough information in a one hour unit of time. This 'nowness' is an operating norm in the urban school.

> Teachers promulgate nowness because, like their students, they are simply try-
> ing to get through each day with the least hassle. Yet, if nowness controls the
> conditions of learning, there is no way to learn any ideas of any consequence
> or develop skills to any high level of proficiency. Education is a process of
> building connections, and this process means hard work for students and
> even harder work for teachers. (1999, p. 3)

Clem understands that he is building more than proficiency in algebra for
DC, but he is engendering better life chances by teaching DC that persistent effort will support him in a future career. Stars understand that real
learning requires an investment of time, determination, and the commitment to overcome hurdles and temporary instructional challenges. This is
the difference between life (quality of life and a career) and death (dropping out, crime, drugs, unemployment, etc.) for the urban learner. "The
principals needed in urban schools serving a majority of at-risk students
believe in students' potential. They must model that generating effort can
make them successful" (p. 37).

Not "Kids at-Risk," but "Kids at-Promise"

The belief in the need for reflection on instructional practice is also a
key component of Mr. Ukoama's philosophy. Clem is a great story teller and
uses colorful metaphors at times to make his point. The hockey metaphor
applies to teaching in the inner city for Clem as he states that "you take a lot
of abuse here . . . it's kind of like hockey . . . you get pushed around and you
have to develop a mentality that helps you to be resilient." He sees reflection as the one ability that allows you to believe and to persist as an educator. The more I talked with Clem it became obvious that he also possesses
this trait and is thoughtful and reflective about his work as a leader.

Clem may be speaking from personal experience when he states that "if
you don't realize you can fail and can't work through your own failures you
won't be any good to anybody . . . that's what allows you to reflect on your practice." This requisite to reflect as an educator, and to adjust your approach in
light of new data and new conditions, is critical to thriving in urban schools
which mimic the changing landscape of American education. And when it
comes to at-risk children, this quality is particularly paramount to success.

Once again, Clem shares a unique perspective on the issue of at-risk children. In his eyes, at-risk children are not "kids at-risk" but "kids at promise."
According to Clem, when you look at your students in this way, "it changes everything . . . if you can turn them around what a great difference you've made."
Again, Clem refers back to his belief system in stating that "you've got to believe
they are worth it all . . . they've lacked so much and been denied so much."
Don't confuse the compassion of Mr. Ukoama with being soft. As we talk, a

[handwritten margin note:] Changing the way you view your students; changes the language you use and how students perceive you.

young student comes to him complaining about tardies and asked Clem to help him with his problem. The answer that student received was soft but firm. Face the music, take your punishment and learn your lesson. To Clem, helping the at-risk child is about understanding them but not about coddling them.

This drive for success for all students is evident in the student achievement results that University Academy has seen under Clem's leadership. Before he arrived at University Academy test scores were ordinary. His time as principal has seen a marked increase in student achievement. In 2006, prior to his arrival, about 25% of the students at University Academy met Missouri's standard of Annual Yearly Progress (AYP) in both mathematics and communication arts. In 2012, this same school had over 90% of their students meeting this same AYP standard. University Academy in 2006 was almost 10 percentage points below the state AYP standard in both mathematics and communication arts. By the 2012 school year, University Academy was more than 10 points above the same state standard of achievement.

Clem gives much of the credit to how he has been able to restructure his school to his training in the Haberman model. He employs a very pragmatic approach to school leadership and realizes that school leaders must "deal with reality and not the picture you have in your head." For example, Clem notes that tests at University Academy are never given during the first period of the school day. Reality for the children of Clem's school is that many come from one parent or dysfunctional homes and that first hour is not the ideal time to ascertain the true learning achieved by these children. Mastery learning also is a part of this belief system as students are given more than one opportunity to learn the material and required to know the material at a higher degree of proficiency.

In Clem's eyes, the work of Dr. Haberman had sensitized people in the profession to the "plight of the at-risk child and to the importance of making special efforts to help them get there." The mastery learning approach and the modified testing schedule at this school were just two tangible examples of the Haberman philosophy on display.

As we ended our talk, Clem took me back to his most basic belief and attributed much of this belief to his training in the Haberman system. For this school leader, you "do what you have to do for your kids." This was the attitude and the belief system that I encountered again and again as I talked to other principals about the Haberman system; and exemplified by Clem.

PRINCIPAL CHRISTIE: GOOD THINGS ARE HAPPENING FOR STUDENTS AT RANDALL ELEMENTARY

Ms. Christy Compton is the principal of Randall Elementary in Independence, Missouri. Christy's background included a stint as a teacher of first and second graders and a time as an instructional coach. Christy is in her seventh year as a principal and her second year as the principal of Randall Elementary. It is worth noting that in her second year in this school district, she is already being recognized for her work in improving student achievement.

Despite her success, Christy is very unassuming and humble in her approach to leadership. My talks with Christy reveal a young lady who is very grateful for the mentors who have given her insight into the art of leadership. She tends to deflect credit to others and sees herself as only a small part in a large operation. This modesty is refreshing but should not hide the fact that Christy is relentless when it comes to student achievement.

 Teachers Save Lives

The student population of Randall Elementary come from families that wrestle many economic challenges. Of the approximately 300 students attending Randall Elementary, almost 275 live in a housing project near the school. This housing project is the largest low income housing project in Missouri. Over 90% of the students in this school are either free or reduced lunch students. Student achievement and attendance have been stubbornly low at this school. Faculty and staff attitudes and comments had been negative about students in the past and Christy Compton shared with me that there was a "laundry list of excuses for why students could not learn" that was shared with her as she began her duties as principal. Haberman (1999) laments,

> If teachers have children failing to learn, there are two options: either something is wrong with the students, or something is wrong with the teacher and his or her methods. Teachers who attribute all the blame to students, their families, and backgrounds may be struggling with their own self concepts. They may be unable to face the reality that they are performing inadequately and must change. They typically create support groups and encourage each other by saying, "They expect us to do everything for the children when there is nothing we can do." (pp. 37–38)

Christy became the heir of a school with very low scores in both communication arts and mathematics on the state assessment tests. Another problem that she inherited was a student body that spent too much time out of class due to misbehavior as determined by their teachers. Teachers at Randall elementary had adopted the practice of just sending their problem students out of their classes and often accused the students, or their home life, for their misbehavior or poor academic performance. But Christy resists blaming the victim and shared with me that the "lowest performing kids are an example of what we are not doing right." The conviction in her voice as she disclosed this key component of her belief system was compelling. Once again, I was reminded of the common attitude that I heard again and again during my research regarding student achievement. Christy counters fatalistic ability thinking of urban learners because she promotes,

> A belief in students' potential to move teachers from blaming the victim to assuming accountability for what and how much children can learn. . . . If the principal believes effort rather than genetic endowment is the best explanation of success in schools, then he or she may be able to change resistant teachers. (p. 38)

Christy believes that "teachers save lives." The teacher that helps a student to improve their reading skills or instructs the struggling learner in mathematics is pulling this disadvantaged student from a world of poverty and failure. Christy had found in Haberman's research the method to find the people she needed to work in her urban school. "Star principals know the effort and costs required to remove weak teachers, or even to improve some of their teaching methods. Consequently, they spend much time and energy on selecting new teachers" (p. 45). For her, the Haberman system of teacher selection gives her a vehicle to use in doing the "most important part of her job . . . the hiring of the right people." She believes that the successful teacher at Randall Elementary must be someone who "can build relationships with kids and teachers that can come into a high need building and make a difference." Christy believes that she and her staff are more than educators. For her, they are involved in a daily battle to save lives and to build a better future for the community by investing in its children.

Christy is insistent that we not talk about any individual student as an example of her success as a leader. She emphasizes that success is a process, not product, of school improvement worth examining. When I press her for an example of a specific form of school improvement that she follows, she is again very emphatic that the best approach to leadership is recursive and adds that leadership does not embody any one approach. Haberman (1999) synthesized the literature on leadership to construct a composite working model from several fields. As a leader, Christy's experiences illuminated instances of these basic principles at work. Star principals understand their role as a leader is to coalesce the stakeholders around a (1) unity of purpose; (2) team building; and (3) commitment to task (p. 31). A star principal "must group and prioritize various perceptions and goals. Once that step has been reached, the principal can lead the constituencies to identify two or three goals that will be the school's highest priorities" (p. 32).

For instance, Christy relies on listening to her teachers and they talk intelligently as a team about several different educational innovations to improve achievement patterns at Randall Elementary. This is a collaborative approach based on the Professional Learning Communities (PLC) to address the curriculum and student achievement issues. In addition, a system of positive behavior supports was implemented to help with the discipline issues. In less than two years a clear pattern of higher student achievement developed and student attendance was up by over 6%. Using an integrated team approach, good things are happening for students at Randall Elementary. Christy's core beliefs personify a practical leadership approach that constantly searches for strategies that will help teachers succeed in order for their students to succeed.

REFLECTION

Star principals who sit on the other side of the desk believe and behave differently from typical principals; they are persistent in their instructional efforts to support learners and see these students as full of promise. My research draws upon interviews conducted with 20 Haberman trained principals. This study has demonstrated that urban principals selected with *The Haberman Star Administrator Selection Interview* tool have beliefs and behaviors that serve as models for other principals. Haberman was a powerful figure behind the success of the 20 principals that I interviewed for my research. These school leaders discovered ideas in the work of Dr. Martin Haberman that inspired and guided them in leading an urban school. Countless comments and accolades were shared with me about the Haberman system and how it had enabled these principals to lead their schools more effectively. It is my quest to expand this research into understanding what makes some principals much more effective than their peers.

My follow-up interviews with Clem and Christie, two of the 20 star principals featured in this chapter, revealed that the Haberman interview system worked for them and echoed the sentiments of their cohort. Clem and Christie did not see the demographics of their school as an excuse for poor student performance but rather as a fact of life that they must directly address. For both Clem and Christy, the key was in developing relationships with students—knowing the demographics or the sad story that accompanies many of their children to school each day was not enough. For school to work for underserved kids, both of these leaders express beliefs and behaviors, from the other side of the desk, through a different lens.

CHAPTER QUESTIONS

1. As you review the list of Haberman's 11 core functions or beliefs (see Chapter 5), rank them in order of importance and give your rationale.

2. Clem was a principal that insisted that students master content. In what way(s) does this act defy a pedagogy of poverty?
3. Haberman explains that blaming the victim is a natural coping device for educationalists. What does he mean by this? Explain a time when you, or an educator you know, blamed the victim. According to Haberman, what can school leaders do to counter this type of deficient or fatalistic belief system in their schools?
4. Christy used PLCs in her school to enhance instruction. How might a new star principal utilize peer or collaborative learning models in a school with resistant teachers, staff, and parents?
5. In what ways have you seen an ideology of unemployment exhibited by teachers in your former or current district? How can leaders develop an action plan for change?

REFERENCES

Haberman, M. (1999). *Star principals serving children in poverty.* Indianapolis, IN: Kappa Delta Pi.

Haberman, M. (2003, Fall). The "star" principal selection interview. *The Haberman Newsletter, 8*(1). Retrieved from http://www.altcert.org/Documents/fall_2003.pdf

Haberman, M. (2004). *Creating effective schools in failed urban districts.* Retrieved from http://www.habermanfoundation.org/Articles/Default.aspx?id=17

CHAPTER 4

STAFFING URBAN PRINCIPALS IN AN ERA OF HYPER-REFORM

A Case from "The Port of Good Things"

Myra I. Whitney
Beverly E. Cross

CHAPTER OBJECTIVES

The learner will

1. Explore a case study of building systemic change in developing effective school leaders;
2. Understand how to interpret and apply the Star Administrator Tools in actual district practice, and;
3. Analyze the impact of strategic leadership selection and development on school reform and student achievement.

The year 2013 marked what many are referring to as 30 years of educational reform in the United States. An analyst on National Public Radio (NPR) stated on April 26, 2013:

Better Principals, Better Schools, pages 49–62
Copyright © 2016 by Information Age Publishing
All rights of reproduction in any form reserved.

Thirty years ago today an alarm sounded in Washington over the state of American education. President Reagan's National Commission on Excellence in Education issued a 65-page report on April 26, 1983. It was titled "A Nation at Risk." The report warned of a rising tide of mediocrity in public schools and launched a wave of education reform.

NPR, scholars, and other media sources recognized three decades of education reform and used their platforms to not only mark this significant moment in the reform movement but also to stimulate what can best be described as a short lived and largely unnoticed marker regarding the benefits and pitfalls to these three decades. These discussions centered on the outcomes of the decades of reform in urban school with particular attention to educational opportunities and equity for the largely poor and minority students who attend these schools. Two large gaps seem to guide these discussions: the gap in student achievement and the gap in America's comparison with other nations. These gaps are analyzed through student achievement data, graduation rates, and dropout rates as markers of the successes and failures of educational reform.

As the pundits talked about the debate on television, in reports, and on the radio, they universally highlighted the key role of teachers as the most critical factor in educational reform and improvement in U.S. schools. They further examined and calculated everything about teachers from their credentials to their performance in what can only be compared to the analysis of sports figures in their performance for the teams that employ them. In many instances they reduced the most important player in education reform, teachers, to a number representing their individual effectiveness. They, likewise, implied that school principals are a vital factor as well but seem to have far less means to document their performance or specify what is needed in effective principals as the march to reform schools continues into decade four. It became evident that while principals are recognized as second in significance in education reform, far less has been done on urban school selection frameworks compared to teachers.

However, Martin Haberman recognized the importance of selecting teachers and principals in his unique approach to staffing urban schools. His framework for selecting Star Teachers and Star Administrators for urban schools defines exactly the dimensions that teachers and principals need to be effective in these most critical educational contexts. Dr. Haberman states "An effective urban school is not led by a principal functioning as a building manager but by an individual functioning as a leader of a non-profit community organization." He further explains three basic goals for these school principal as (1) creating a common vision; (2) building effective teams to implement the vision; and (3) engendering commitment to the task (i.e., the persistent hard work needed to engender learning).

THE CONTEXT

Some researchers and educators distinguish educational reform levels of intensity as ranging from little reform on one end of the continuum to hyper reform at the other end. Memphis is engaged in what can only be classified as hyper reform. Memphis is the 23rd largest school district in the Nation with over 200 schools and approximately 7,000 teachers. Beginning in 2008, the new superintendent and deputy superintendent led the district in identifying several fault lines which they believed would determine whether the district would improve its performance as a system or remain as what Dr. Haberman refers to as one of "The 120 largest school districts in the United States in which greater size correlates with greater failure and the miseducation of thousands of children." Further, Memphis is often referred to as a key ground zero site of today's education reform movement. For example, during the year between May, 2012 and May, 2013, Education Week includes Memphis in 84 stories. The school district has achieved this degree of analysis due to its hyper reform status stimulated by being awarded Race to the Top funding, Bill and Melinda Gates funding, and the merger of the city school system with the area county school district that represents the surrounding suburbs. These are all systemic-level reforms that have the potential to achieve what school reform has as a key guide: improving educational performance for all students and, especially in urban contexts, the performance of minority children in poverty (the very children and youth Dr. Haberman dedicated a lifetime of work to).

We focus on the key role of principals in this hyper-reform context. Alongside the six fault lines and the massive effort to improve teacher effectiveness aligned with Race to the Top and the Gates Funding, the then superintendent perceptively recognized that what the district lacked was a strong "bench" of effective school leaders to serve as instructional leaders in the schools. This sports metaphor highlighted the game changing roles of school leaders in ameliorating the fault lines and reforming the district. The shortage of effective principals was, in essence, an unstated seventh fault line that had to be reconciled for the reform work to be significant in improving the entire district. The superintendent commissioned the Associate Superintendent of Professional Development, Myra I. Whitney, to design a new model for principal selection and development that closed the gap in the preparedness of the principals based on the fact that they were trained by various higher education institutions and groups such as New Leaders for New Schools (as they were named at that time). He called for school leaders to become instructional leaders with a shared understanding of the district mission and values, accountability, district-wide data, key district initiatives, and turning around low and underperforming schools. He wanted the school leaders to have a shared knowledge base and to develop the skills to lead the schools to become high performing, focused on learning and achievement, and who saw education as many others did, the civil rights issue of our time. This required attention to the selection of school leaders and their preparation.

In response to this high-stakes clarion call, Myra I. Whitney in 2008, conceived of and launched the National Urban Education Center (UEC) for the Memphis City Schools with the idea that it would be the home of an innovative strategy for preparing school leaders. The mission statement for the UEC is to "Develop transformational urban leaders with a sense of urgency and innovation to ensure overall student success." A secondary mission was to "Grow your own program for leaders who would know the district's values and mission." To assure the approach would be innovative and aligned with leadership preparation and practices outside of education, she established a broad, cross-sector advisory board in 2009. This 12-member board represented representatives from the corporate community, higher education, K–12 education, and the non-profit community. These established leaders in the community in collaboration with the local Chamber of Commerce and the Southern Regional Education Board developed the Executive Leadership Program (ELP) which develops and supports aspiring school leaders. The diversity and richness of the expertise and perspectives on leadership from across these sectors contributed substantially to creating a stronger program. These education and community leaders were driven by an outcomes based leadership program and recognized that a strong, proven selection strategy was a necessary prerequisite to assuring the effectiveness of the ELP and the impact of the program on producing high-performing school leaders. This chapter reports on the selection strategy, its place in the broader process for preparing principals, and the preliminary outcomes and impact generated as a result.

SELECTING ASPIRING SCHOOL LEADER CANDIDATES

Many in education recognize and struggle with the ageless debate over whether screening and selecting aspiring future educators and principals is the key fundamental initial step in their preparation for America's classrooms and schools or whether program preparation is the leading indicator of who will be successful. In either case, the answer is not totally selection or preparation but disputes continue around, which is the top priority. A key fundamental principle guiding the Star Administrator according to Haberman is selection. He states, "Potential star principals must be selected. That is, individuals who already hold the ideology that characterizes star principals can benefit from subsequent training and learn the effective behaviors.' He explains that the ideology is a "value laden system of beliefs *caught* and developed by life experiences rather than taught in graduate courses of school administration" (1999, p. xi). With this in mind, a significant amount of attention must be given to selecting aspiring principals and then designing an innovative program to develop their knowledge and skills to be effective in urban schools. In general, across education settings individuals are tapped to become a school leader by an area superintendent, a fellow principal, other district leaders, or other politics or bureaucratic processes that may not be directly guided by student learning expectations. Haberman describes these "real world" criteria to appoint principals are often based on their ability to control the building, be loyal, insulate higher administration by containing problems, be an educational leader focused on keeping a lid on the school and supporting the administration, and being able to communicate well to stakeholders. Using these criteria, traditional selection then assures the potential school leaders obtain their principal license through an area university, through New Leaders for New Schools, and through individual state departments of education. Thus, the school leadership pool or bench has vastly different understandings, values, beliefs, skills, knowledge, commitments, and expectations. This situation in Memphis led the superintendent to accurately conclude that a strong bench did not exist to draw from to identify leaders for a district operating in hyper educational reform. The severity of this situation led to what is referred to here as the seventh unnamed fault line that represents a serious weakness to turning around an urban school system—school leaders.

Considering the exigency of leadership development in the landscape of the district's work, the associate superintendent presented the superintendent and the board of education with a plan to use the Haberman School Administrator Pre-Screener and Interview Protocol as the initial step in identifying aspiring school leaders. The Haberman Principal Selection tools received approval largely because of their focus on urban school leaders and the dimensions of effective urban school leadership assessed through the online pre-screener and the interview, which assess the values and beliefs that are prerequisite dispositions to other knowledge and skill training. The dimensions listed in Table 4.1 assess the values and beliefs that support smart selection of aspiring school leaders. We will explain later how we used the Star Administrator dimensions to not only select aspiring leaders but subsequently to guide the knowledge and skill training in the ELP program as well.

A new district policy required that everyone seeking to become a principal or assistant principal must be first screened using the Haberman Online Pre-Screener followed by the Haberman interview. The use of the Haberman Star Administrator tools with a focus on the dimensions identified above aligned with the district's commitment to staffing schools with leaders prepared to lead in complex urban school environments, thus became

TABLE 4.1 List of Haberman Dimensions of Effective Urban School Leadership

Star Principals vs Traditional Principals are contrasted as:
  Sensitive to Diversity/Insensitive to Diversity
  Creates a Common Vision/Fosters Personal Preferences
  Develops Positive Working Climate/Enforces Rules
  Instructional Leader/Building Manager
  Data Driven/Idiosyncratic
  Product Evaluation/Process Evaluation
  Personal Accountability/Others Accountability
  Responsible Leader/Delegator
  Expanded Principal's Role/Traditional Principal's Role
  Bottom-Up Representative/Top-Down Representative
  Parents with Voice/Parents as Helpers
  Client Advocate/Staff Advocate
  Problem Solver/Reactor

the initial screen in the selection process for aspiring school leaders. In effect, these research-based, proven tools replaced the criteria Haberman identified as current practice in many urban school districts (e.g., loyalty or ability to keep a lid on the school). The rigorous, comprehensive application and selection process for school leaders involved a day-long process that included several components beyond the traditional expectations of years of experience, advanced degrees and state licensure. To apply, interested applicants to the ELP were required to complete the following:

- Initial Screening through the Haberman Online Pre-Screener
- Interview using the Haberman Star Administrator Protocol
- Data Analysis Assessment using a Case Study
- Writing Assessment

In addition to assessing the Haberman dimensions of school administrators through the Pre-Screener and the Interview, that data analysis and writing were used to identify the following attributes in applicants: (1) instructional knowledge/expertise; (2) commitment to continuous learning; (3) professional resilience; (4) strong communication skills; (5) professional integrity; and (6) willingness/ability to be self-reflective.

This application process required that the professional development staff, the Human Resources Staff, the four area superintendents, and selected university faculty be trained to conduct the Haberman interview. Once trained by the Haberman Foundation, this cadre conducted interviews of each future leader and made decisions about who would enter the Executive Leadership Program—the innovative approach to preparing school leaders for Memphis City Schools discussed below.

Developing School Leaders

Although the primary aim of the Star Administrator tools is to support urban school districts in the selection of school leaders, we also saw them as useful in the program's curriculum. To us, the dimensions articulated in the framework are powerful to not only select aspiring leader candidates but also to continue their development for our schools. We understood that alignment in selection, development, and assessment would enable us to have stronger, focused leaders because of the consistency that would result from this alignment. Therefore, we continued the use of the Star Administrator dimensions into the program for preparing school leaders through the Executive Leadership Program. This, we believe, is a unique contribution to the curriculum developed and implemented in Memphis's Executive Leadership Program.

The Executive Leadership Program (ELP) takes a comprehensive, competency-based approach to improving the quality of education for students by developing a cadre of school leaders committed to eliminating the achievement gap. The ELP is designed to address the critical need for quality leaders in urban schools and utilizes a teaching hospital concept that employs a recursive process for problem analysis, knowledge application, diagnosis, strategy development, treatment, and outcome analysis (www.mcsk12.net/pd/uec). The teaching hospital concept is more than metaphorical for the work in Memphis and seemed particularly relevant considering Dr. Haberman's recent analysis of most urban schools as miseducating to death the children of color and in poverty that attend them. He stated:

> Fourteen million diverse children in poverty are currently being miseducated. The seven million in urban poverty (disproportionately represented by children of color), attend school in the 120 largest school districts. By many accounts, these districts are failing school systems in which greater size correlates positively with greater failure. Every miseducated child represents a personal tragedy. Each will have a lifelong struggle to ever have a job that pays enough to live in a safe neighborhood, have adequate health insurance, send their own children to better schools than they went to, or have a decent retirement. In most cases their lives are limited to dead end jobs or wasted away in street violence or prison. Living in the midst of the most prosperous nation on earth, the miseducated will live shorter, less healthy lives characterized by greater stress and limited life options. Miseducation is, in effect, a sentence of death carried out daily over a lifetime. It is the most powerful example I know of cruel and unusual punishment and it is exacted on children innocent of any crime. (Haberman, 2007, p. 180)

We set out to design a program that was purposeful in not only eliminating the achievement gap as we mentioned earlier, but also in stopping the death sentence caused by poor educational opportunity. We wanted to select and develop leaders based on the belief that "School leadership is the process of putting the best interests of the school's children ahead of the convenience of the adults" (Haberman, 1999, p. 15).

With the guidance of the cross-sector advisory board, the Chamber of Commerce, the Haberman Star Administrator dimensions, a site visit to the New York Leadership Academy, the Southern Education Regional Board (SREB), the Tennessee Instructional Leadership Standards (TILS), and the Interstate School Leaders Licensure Consortium (ISLLC) standards, the program to develop school leaders was successfully designed. Each Phase of the program includes online and face-to-face instructional practices that employ cases, problems, clinical sites, and a residency component. The program phases are shown in Figure 4.1.

Aspiring leaders who successfully complete the four-part screening and selection process participate in the four phases of the program. During *Phase I*, the aspiring leaders engage in a problem based, action learning curriculum that simulates the challenges of an urban principalship. *Phase II* is conducted utilizing experienced principal mentors along with core curriculum modules. *Phase III* enables aspiring leaders to transition successfully into school leadership positions. During the planning summer preceding school placements, the newly assigned school leaders apply their program learning to their new school contexts. They analyze their schools' student achievement data, school leadership, and culture. They must also create a professional development plan for their year as a school leader. During *Phase IV*, the school leaders work and learn with mentors who provide extensive, on-going support that carries over three years. It is important to note that that support system for the aspiring school leaders and novice school leaders include mentors (exemplary principals from across the nation such as New York, Ohio, Illinois) who provide support for novice principals; leadership fellows who provide site visits and virtual coaching

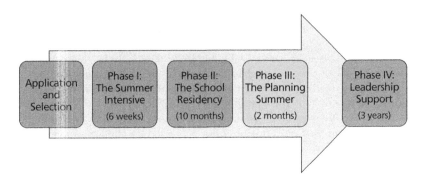

Figure 4.1 The executive leadership program phases and timeline.

throughout the program; district coaches who lead intensive sessions and provide onsite academic mentors for the novice principals; and sessions from the SREB Learning-Centered Leadership Program. In addition, some of the novice principals attend the Harvard Principal Institute, visit the New York City Leadership Academy, and complete 360 degree assessment and the NYCLA Leadership Performance Planning Worksheet.

These supports align with the strategic framework for the competency-based design of the program and the program competencies listed below. Table 4.2 shows the critical alignment of the ELP competencies with the Star Administrator Dimensions. The left-hand column lists the ELP competencies, the middle column provides a brief summary of the outcomes expected for leaders to perform, and the right-hand column indicates the Star Administrator dimensions that align with the ELP competencies and outcomes. The alignment is significant in that it carries the Star Administrator Dimensions forward from screening and selection to program design and content. As a consequence, aspiring leaders in the ELP program are not only screened and selected for the program but are also assessed throughout the program and exit the program based on these dimensions.

These competencies are translated into a detailed, finely nuanced rubric that is used to guide the development of the aspiring school leaders and to assess their preparedness to enter leadership positions. Based on their summative assessment, program completers are identified as exemplary,

TABLE 4.2   Analysis of Executive Leadership Program and Haberman Star Administrator Dimensions

ELP Competency	Competency Outcome	Haberman Star Administrator Dimensions
Mission and Orientation	The school leader acts as an advocate for rigorous standards for all students along with their social and emotional development as the mission of the school	Creates a common vision rather than personal preferences Bottom up representative rather than top-down representative
Culture and Climate	The school leaders creates and sustains an ethical, diverse, equitable and collaborative environment for students, staff, parents and communities that protects and maximized quality learning	Develops positive working climate rather than enforces rules
Diversity	The school leader addresses cultural expectations in all dimensions of the school from interactions, policies, curriculum, and collaborations	Sensitive to Diversity rather than insensitive to diversity

(continued)

TABLE 4.2 Analysis of Executive Leadership Program and Haberman Star Administrator Dimensions (Continued)

ELP Competency	Competency Outcome	Haberman Star Administrator Dimensions
Youth Development	The school leader invests in youth capacity building through various supports that align with the complexity of youth and their learning, imagination, thinking and developmental needs	Client advocate rather than staff advocate
Professional Growth and Development	The school leader provides leadership in preparing educators to positively impact student learning and models continuous learning and collaboration	Addressed in Haberman's focus on school leaders as continuous learners
Accountability/ System-wide Performance	The school leader collects, analyzes, and uses data to make professional decisions, to prioritize improvements and practices, and to communicate with different stakeholders to benefit student learning	Personal accountability rather than holding only others accountable
Technology	The school leader promotes and supports technology as a learning tool and uses it in communicating with various stakeholders	Addressed by Haberman as a key role for instructional leaders
Research and Standards-Based Curriculum and Instruction	The school leader creates a comprehensive, rigorous and coherent curricular and instructional program and monitors, assesses and reports on student learning and progress	Data driven rather than idiosyncratic Product evaluation rather than process evaluation
Transformational Leadership and Innovation	The school leader is guided by a vision of learning, manages change, collaborates with stakeholders, and facilitates continuous school improvement	Expanded principal's role rather than traditional principal's role Parents with voice rather than parents as helpers Problem solver rather than reactor
Professional Ethics	The school leader performs with integrity and fairness and is accountable for student success and development	Responsible leader rather than delegator
Financial/ Operations	The school leader while focused on student success and achievement daily, also ensures management of the organization for efficiency to support that mission	Addressed through Haberman's focus on the unique urban context and bureaucracy

professional, beginning, or aspiring leaders. Further, each competency is assessed using authentic data, evidence, and cases that support the hospital teaching model used as a framework for the program. Aspiring leaders complete the program through a final exhibition of skills based on a rubric that assesses: (1) effective oral presentation skills; (2) logical and effective organization in presenting; (3) effective use of visual aids; (4) effective use of data and research; (5) ability to identify problems and propose solutions; and (6) mastery of MCS leadership skills.

EARLY INSIGHTS FROM MEMPHIS

The ELP just marked the completion of its fifth graduating cohort as this chapter is being written in spring, 2013. We have a great deal to learn and will continue the work and study its impact over time in a systematic way. The following, however, mark a few insights we are gleaning from the program.

We begin our report of key learnings with student achievement because that is the purpose of screening, selection, and program curriculum (Roberts, 2012).

- Elementary schools led by the program graduates have demonstrated an increase in student achievement by 14%
- High schools led by program graduates have improved English student achievement scores by an average of 5.9% and Algebra I by 5%
- Six schools led by ELP graduates have been recognized as EPIC Award winning schools
- Three schools led by ELP graduates have been awarded the Tennessee Reward Schools

Second, a key goal of the ELP is to increase the bench of school leaders with a shared urban education knowledge base and district mission and values. The following evidence demonstrates how this bench is not only being developed but also utilized in various leadership capacities in the district:

- Demand remains high for the program with nearly 1,500 applications
- 144 of the applications met the rigorous admission standards, which included the Star Administrator Pre-Screener and Interview
- The program has graduated 142 aspiring school leaders
- 81 ELP graduates have taken school leadership positions: 36 as principals and 40 as assistant principals
- A few ELP graduates hold central office positions

Third, the Executive Leadership program has been recognized for its innovation in developing aspiring, high performing leaders as evidenced by:

- A competitive grant award from the USDOE School Leadership Grant and the Tennessee Department of Education Principal Residency Grant (the only principal residency grant awarded in the state)
- Identified by the Wallace Foundation as a promising practice in the School Leadership Pipeline Initiative
- Presentations accepted at national and international conferences including the Council of Great City Schools and Learning Forward

CONCLUSIONS

While the outcomes and impacts may appear moderate, they offer promise for a five-year old program in improving the selection, development, and performance of aspiring school leaders in an urban school district. They also show a trajectory of turning around schools with attention on leadership as a key strategy of improving student outcomes.

The program has several important implications for the use of the Star Administrator tools in urban school contexts. In 2008, the National Bureau of Economic Research conducted a study on effective teachers, which was led by a team of scholars from Columbia University, Harvard Graduate School of Education, the University of Michigan, and Dartmouth College. As part of their study, they investigated the Haberman Star Teacher Evaluation Pre-Screener (similar to the Pre-Screener used in the Memphis approach to select aspiring school leaders). They concluded the following from their investigation:

> We find statistically significant but modest relationships between student achievement and several non-traditional predictors of teacher effectiveness, including performance on the Haberman selection instrument. We find marginally significant increases of about 0.02 standard deviations in math achievement associated with one-standard deviation increases in cognitive ability and self-efficacy. For respondents' scores on a test of math knowledge for teaching, we estimate an effect size of about 0.03 standard deviations and statistical significance at the 2 percent level. Scores on the Haberman Pre-Screener are also positively related to student achievement, with an effect size of 0.02 standard deviations, which is marginally significant at the 11 percent level. (Rockoff, Jacob, Kane, & Staiger, 2008)

We cite this study here even though it focuses on teachers because similar research has not been conducted on the school administrator Pre-Screener. But this study was significant in our decision to require the Haberman

Pre-Screener and Interview and we believe as the long-term evaluation continues, it will positively relate to student achievement for school leaders in a similar manner as it does for teachers.

Further research cites teacher retention for those selected using the Haberman tools to be between 95% and 98% compared to studies conducted over the past two decades that found between 40% and 50% of new teachers leaving within their first five years of teaching and another 45–50% leaving after four years. Teacher retention is so important because it is held to be a primary factor in the unequal education of children from urban and poor communities. In addition, a study conducted of Star Teachers found that of those who completed the program between 1990 and 1999, "94% are still teaching in Milwaukee Public Schools" and 100% are still teaching. We believe similar retention of principals is critically important and can have long-term positive implications for educational opportunity for urban schools and for the reforms that can lead to better educational opportunities.

Memphis City Schools is in the process of creating a principal's effectiveness measure similar to its teacher effectiveness measure. When data are available regarding the effectiveness of principals from this measure, we are hopeful to show results that are predictive from using the Haberman tools.

One of the meanings of the word Memphis is the "Port of Good Things." We share this case of reform and innovation in urban school leadership as part of a larger national conversation about improving education. This is not a simple, naïve victory case, but rather an example of one city's story to enact important school reform. Student achievement has improved over the past three years. Our local newspaper reported in 2012, that Memphis is "making some of the largest strides ever according to the state report card . . . but failed to close the achievement gap." Thus, this case explains our work, our successes, and the challenge that we still face as we attempt to turn around urban schools and the district. And although we have a great deal more to study and learn as the work progresses, we are hopeful based on the initial data that we can continue to share the work from the Port of Good Things.

CHAPTER QUESTIONS

1. What factors would your district have to consider in designing a "grow your own" program in light of the standards and expectations set out by ISLLC and your state? What would a matrix of alignment look like for you?
2. Who are the key stakeholders in your community that should be involved in designing school leadership programs? Why should each be present and what do they uniquely bring to the process?

3. What are the educational gaps that exist in your district? Identify the relevant skills and knowledge principals in your district need to eliminate any educational gaps that exists.
4. How are school leaders currently identified, screened and selected in your district? How has that changed over time and what could lead to the selection of instructional leaders instead?
5. What are some key turning points (both positive and negative) in the Memphis case that you want to pay particular attention in your district's work?

REFERENCES

Haberman, M. (1999). *Increasing the number of high-quality African American teachers in urban schools.* Retrieved from http://www.habermanfoundation.org/Articles/Default.aspx?id=66

Haberman, M. (2007). Who benefits from failing urban schools? An essay. *Theory into Practice, 46*(3), 179–186.

Roberts, J. (2012, November 1). *Report card shows gains in Memphis, Shelby County Schools.* Memphis, TN: The Commercial Appeal.

Rockoff, J. E., Jacob, B. A., Kane, T. J., & Staiger, D. O. (2008, November). *Can you recognize an effective teacher when you recruit one?* Cambridge, MA: National Bureau of Economic Research.

CHAPTER 5

THE CASE FOR SELECTING BETTER PRINCIPALS

Valerie Hill-Jackson
Delia Stafford

There are three imperatives for this book. First, Haberman explained that the problem with school leadership is a result of *selection blindness*; districts are unaware that current default interview models are misguided and repeatedly fail to identify suitable school leaders. The Haberman Star Administrator Selection Instrument (HSASI) tool (also known as the Haberman Administrator Pre-Screener) is proven, through evidence-based practice, to harvest better principals for turnaround schools. The choice of the right personnel to staff schools, to ensure that each student succeeds, is one of the cornerstones of Haberman's life work. His vision of a star principal for every school is based on the belief that selection of the right principal "up front" is even more important than training.

Second, the achievement gap between 15 million children in poverty in the United States, and their mainstream counterparts, continues to widen. Nearly 50% of school-aged students are children of color, 21% speak a language other than English at home, and one in five of all public schools are high poverty schools (NCES, 2014). Increasingly, principals are being challenged to raise academic standards and graduation rates among students

Better Principals, Better Schools, pages 63–79
Copyright © 2016 by Information Age Publishing
All rights of reproduction in any form reserved.

who are ethnically, politically, linguistically, economically, religiously, or geo-graphically diverse. Haberman surmised that 'highly qualified urban school districts' are unicorns, as he discovered that an elevated percentage of ad-ministrators are underprepared to work effectively with faculty and impov-erished students. All of us absorbed by processes to scale-up the numbers of successful leaders are interested in knowing why some principals are stars while others still struggle—a formula must exist for determining the traits of talented principals. Haberman (1999) proposes 11 mid-range functions for administrators: (1) leadership; (2) commitment to student learning; (3) the-ory into practice; (4) role of the school serving students in poverty; (5) cur-riculum and instructional leadership; (6) creating a positive school climate and fighting burnout; (7) evaluation/accountability; (8) decision making; (9) fallibility; (10) administrative style; and (11) administrative relations with parents and community. These competencies are worth investigating further since nascent research validates the link between effective leaders and school achievement among underserved learners (Branch, Hanushek, & Rivkin, 2009; The Wallace Foundation, 2012). The logical next step is to revisit the HSASI, which fills this knowing-doing gap, and engenders principals who can champion on behalf of underserved learners in at-risk schools and districts.

Third, practitioners and researchers need exemplars which demonstrate the functions of dynamic principals. For those who ask, 'yeah, but how do you cre-ate better principals and what do better schools look like', this volume answers those questions. School leaders, who have successfully used the HSASI, provide inside perspectives that illustrate the *"better principals, better schools"* clarion call.

This chapter is divided into four parts and begins by deciphering the social, political and research landscape of the principalship in general, and the challenges of the urban school principal in particular, in our fluid soci-ety. Next, a star principal believes in one overarching philosophy—leader-ship for social justice. So a recap of the standards and ideology for the tra-ditional principalship is placed in stark contrast to the twenty-first century star principal model which Haberman exhorts. The editors assert that star principals can be located by getting to the root of what they believe because administrative actions are dictated by one's core beliefs. Then, the research and development of the HSASI questionnaire is shared. For decades the HSASI has been repeatedly implemented and honed, through an iterative research procedure, to become a value-added mechanism for principal se-lection. Finally, the chapter closes with a brief summation.

PREPARING PRINCIPALS FOR A CHANGING WORLD

Now, more than ever, principals must straddle dual missions; objectives which are focused on student achievement and their responsibilities as conventional managers with a public persona (Lortie, 2009). The principal must serve three masters—the general uniformed public who want results yesterday; teacher unions, superintendents and boards who are disconnected from the main stakeholders; and teachers, parent groups and students who are on the front lines of educational investments and outcomes (Fenwick & Pierce, 2001).

Today's focus on understanding the instructional leadership is relatively new. Following the effective schools movement of the 1980s and 1990s, a growing interest in principal leadership emerged (Hallinger, 2015). Today, an expanding literature album has advanced in the twenty-first century around developing school leaders, including: preparation and training (McCarthy, 2002; McCarthy, 2005; McCarthy & Forsyth, 2009; Orr, 2006); best practices (Darling-Hammond, LaPointe, Meyerson, Orr, & Cohen, 2007); responsibilities (Waters, Marzano & McNulty, 2004) shifting role (Browne-Ferrigno, 2003; Davis, Darling-Hammond, LaPointe, & Meyerson, 2005; Lortie, 2009); and effectiveness (Beteille, Kalogrides, & Loeb 2011; Coelli & Green, 2012; Miller, 2013). Further, the latest school reform efforts are forcing here-to-day-gone-tomorrow mandates on districts for reporting which principals are "highly effective," "effective," and "ineffective" (Center for Public Education, 2012). Only recently have we come to understand the impending principal staffing crisis (Fenwick & Pierce, 2001; Hammond, Muffs, & Sciascia, 2001; Lovely, 2004) as something more disturbing than a dwindling pool of prospective principals. A more nuanced review of the literature on principal leadership shortages exposes that the problem is more complex than an inadequate supply to meet demand. States generally certify more than enough administrators to fill principal vacancies and most open positions receive multiple applications. Despite this excess pool of individuals certified to be administrators, there remains an excess demand for school administrators, in part because many certified individuals are not choosing to pursue school leadership positions but more importantly because the demand is for a new type of principal—one with attributes and abilities beyond simply the possession of an appropriate administrative credential. Consequently, *districts are not facing a labor shortage, as much as a skills shortage*—characterized by the inability to fill school leadership positions with people who possess the skills necessary to be successful. This shortage may partially result from insufficient compensation for school leaders; however, the shortage could also stem from the recruitment and selection processes districts utilize (cited in Myung, Loeb, & Horng, 2011, pp. 696–697, emphasis added).

The crisis of principal supply is, at best, misunderstood and, at worst, manufactured. While there are several states that wrestle with recruitment and attrition among school leadership (e.g., Illinois, Maryland, and Ohio), Haberman explains that the real principal crisis is not concerned with whether we have enough leaders (Pounder, Galvin, & Shepard, 2003; Roza, 2003), but whether or not we have enough leaders who embody the knowledge, skills, and core beliefs of the futurist principal for struggling school districts.

The Challenge of School Leadership in Hard-to-Staff Schools

School districts are struggling to find public school leaders who have these intricate requisites to become stellar principals, especially in hard-to-staff schools. Hard-to-staff schools are defined as schools with high minority student populations, with low test scores, in high poverty communities. Recent research has shown that urban school principals have an even greater impact on student achievement than principals in less challenging schools. The constructive direction of a superior school leader is not limited to academics but has far-reaching consequences on teacher performance and turnover. Additionally, many studies argue the positive connection between quality principals and student academic outcomes since principals impact various student outcomes beyond test scores:

- School attendance was positively impacted by effective school principals in all schools ranging from low-performing, high-poverty to high-achieving, low-poverty schools. However, the impact was even greater in the former as opposed to the latter; and
- Graduation rates also positively impacted by effective principals in sustained roles. A graduation rate of nearly three percentage points is attributed to highly effective principals compared to their average counterparts. (cited in Center for Public Education, 2012)

To be sure, the responsibilities of the principal are not limited to school suspensions or teacher schedules, but woven into a multi-layered process for understanding student and school outcomes. Sergiovanni (1996a; 1996b) evaluates that this revised archetype of the principal also includes motivating, maintaining harmony, sharing the vision, institutionalizing values, managing, explaining, modeling, enabling, and supervising school stakeholders. The importance of understanding the school leader's style, as a direct and indirect influence on the school, is weighty since there is a high correlation between principal functions and school performance.

IT'S WHAT YOU BELIEVE THAT COUNTS: RETHINKING THE PRINCIPAL'S FUNCTIONS

In 1996, the Interstate School Leaders Licensure Consortium (ISLLC) created a set of standards for determining the competencies of school leaders. ISLLC is a consortium of national education leadership organizations including the National Association of Elementary School Principals, the National Association of Secondary School Principals, the National Policy Board on Educational Administration, and the Council of Chief State School Officers. In 2008, the six standards were revised to describe the behaviors of school leaders who should be:

- Stewards of a shared vision;
- Advocates, nurturers, and sustainers of a school culture and instructional program conducive to student learning and professional growth;
- Managers of the organization, operations, and resources for a safe, efficient, and effective learning environment;
- Collaborators with faculty and community members, responding to diverse community interests and needs, and mobilizing community resources;
- Actors of integrity, exercising fairness and in an ethical manner; and
- Responders to, and influencers of, the political, social, economic, legal, and cultural context. (Council of Chief State School Officers, 2008)

The ISLLC standards are a broad set of nationally recognized principles, informed by decades of studies, and used as a template in local districts for developing or updating their own benchmarks for preparing and identifying principals. To the casual observer, these six criteria provide a research-based yardstick by which to measure the overall effectiveness of school leaders. However, Haberman (1999; 2001) finds that these standards are incomplete and warrant a more critical exploration for the functions of school leaders with social justice ideologies.

Several of Haberman's key functions for the star principal overlap with the competencies of ISLLC's traditional principal in that both recognize that school leaders must: (1) develop, communicate, and live the mission; (2) have a deep knowledge about teaching and learning; and (3) build and maintain collaborative relationships. Haberman (2001) inserts two additional functions central to being an effective school leader: (4) create and sustain accountable systems; and (5) understand and manage change (p. 23). Haberman explains that school leaders cannot be effective in the first four areas unless they understand change and the challenges to managing it. As a star with an ideology bent toward equity and fairness, the principal performs and thinks like a futurist by integrating all five areas of this model in the face of district reforms and restructuring. For Haberman, this requires the school principal to serve as a change agent; one who can concentrate on twenty-first century demands with moral fortitude.

Principled Principals: School Leadership for Social Justice

Haberman's critical perspective on the economic, social, and educational barriers imposed upon underserved learners in America is derived from an overarching ideology of school leadership for social justice. Social justice is an idea of equitable learning experiences for marginalized learners (Goldfarb & Grinberg, 2002) and it is connected to practices that ensure equitable results, in the face of change and resistance, by those in leadership positions (Bogotch, 2002). Star principals sponsor education that attends to the many divergent needs of learners from various cultural backgrounds. They understand that opportunities for learners are based on a flawed concept of meritocracy. Stars know the world is not fair and many students have the equivalent of a zip code education—learning experiences determined by their students' community and financial resources. Star principals have already calculated the horrible self-fulfilling prophecy for their learners and work long hours to prove the educational predictions wrong. Stars with an ideology of social justice refuse to accept the normative agenda in education. They advocate that,

> Marginalized students do not receive the education they deserve unless purposeful steps are taken to change schools on their behalf with both equity and justice consciously in mind.... Administrators must be at the front of the line in transforming schools into more equitable and just places. With this social justice purpose clearly in mind, enacting resistance requires that future administrators develop a reflective consciousness centered on social justice and a broader knowledge and skill base. Developing reflective consciousness contains four components that can be marshaled to enact resistance and lead toward social justice:
>
> 1. Learning to believe the dream is possible,
> 2. Models of equity and justice in practice,
> 3. Deepening administrators' knowledge of self, and
> 4. Rebellious, oppositional imaginations. (cited in Theoharis, 2007, p. 250)

Star principals see their job as lead learner and recognize that creating nurturing, educative learning environments, for children living on society's fringe, as an ethical obligation. Stars grasp that a good education for the underserved is the difference between life (positive post-secondary education experiences, worthwhile employment, and contributing as a member of society) and death (elevated high-school drop-outs, drug abuse, un/underemployment, jail, etc.). Sergiovanni (1996c) concurs and calls for activist practices in leadership, which can transform a school from an organization to a community, with moral foundation built around purpose, values, and beliefs.

Superintendents hire school leaders and they typically are not interested in the aims of social justice that, on the surface, are not directly beneficial for the district. Instead, they seek administrative qualities and status quo perspectives that serve the district's needs. What's worse, most principals incorrectly adopt these outlooks as their own. Such conceptions of *control, loyalty, insulation, leadership, and communication* are highly valued commodities of the principal from the superintendent's point of view. The star principal embodies these characteristics, not just in a way that is advantageous to the leadership, but for the learners and community as well. Haberman (1999) explains that being a successful school executive requires something more than traits and characteristics which can be feigned; that something more is an orientation toward social justice. It is what a principal believes that ultimately determines star leadership that can turn schools around. The superficial qualities that interviewers look for in prospective candidates—such as communication, school culture, decision making, and so forth—can be learned or mimicked and their beliefs are susceptible to changing at the whim and pleasure of school boards and superintendents. These characteristics exist on the edge of one's temperament and do not reflect the core of the individual. Principals who have core beliefs, anchored in futurist and social justice worldviews or ideologies, exercise the characteristics of the principal to the benefit of the stakeholders and disenfranchised

Star principals believe that:

- Leadership requires collaboration and hard work to communicate a persistent and focused vision embedded in the needs of stakeholders; student learning is at the center of their work and will remove any obstacles toward that goal;
- Bad teachers are detrimental to the academic health of learners and schools and they are directly involved in the selection and placement of teachers;
- Ideas drive practice and practice drives ideas;
- A wide variety of family services must be connected by schools to families, or even delivered in school sites linked with community health and service providers because they believe in educating the whole child. Star principals know and engage the curriculum, seek best instructional practices, know instructional strategies, and engage the academic life of the school
- Safety and security are more than brick and mortar issues, but are measures of the stakeholders' emotional health and includes feelings of collegiality, acceptance, and affirmation—even guests are made to feel like dignitaries;
- All roads of accountability, good and bad, lead to them;

- Distributive leadership is best for the decision making process and steer the stakeholders to remain focused on student success in the midst of national and state reforms;
- Stars are the first people in the school to admit when they are wrong because they know that fallibility is a sign of strength, not weakness;
- Stakeholders need leaders who can help them act in their best interests so they don't ask stakeholders what they can do for them, but how can they can serve the stakeholders, and;
- Parents, caregivers, and community are instrumental to student learning.

There are competing ideologies that separate the beliefs and behaviors of the average principal from the star principal (see Table 5.1, *Traditional vs. Star Principals' Beliefs about Haberman's Mid-Range Functions*). The traditional principal believes that: leadership is an insular endeavor and they become stewards to a flappable vision—mandates are the gospel in times of erratic, high-speed reform; due to a principal's expanded school duties, teacher selection and placement should be deferred to human resources—they lack foresight into how teacher quality impacts student achievement; traditional principals draw from a scant knowledge base on the craft of the principalship; status quo principals believe that schools are not proxies of social services because they are primarily focused on the cognitive, not affective domain of learning; they rationalize their lack of instructional prowess with such comments like 'teachers are born and not made' and 'the union won't let me fire anybody'; discipline and routine are more important than relationships and stakeholder rewards; high-stakes testing is a product, not a process and they cannot imagine other ways to assess their performance; decision making is hierarchical; one should never own up to a mistake; stakeholders behave and interact in schools at the pleasure of the principal; and the voices of the community and have little to no value. These invisible, destructive beliefs undermine effective hiring prices and bolster the *selection blindness* phenomenon.

Schools need star principals whose beliefs are stakeholder-centered and intractable. The manner in which any human being behaves in any role is really a function of what s/he believes. The inspection of a principal's core beliefs has failed to receive the same type of scrutiny as the established attributes for school leaders that can be easily mimicked or learned for a licensure exam. Many examine the work of principals through an outdated prism—some sort of applied science connected to an unflinching research-focused knowledge base, but the reality is that the principal's work is much more craft-like and artistic (Schlechty, 2001; Sergiovanni, 2001). Finding individuals who exhibit Haberman's 11 mid-range functions involves a highly

TABLE 5.1 Traditional vs. Star Principals' Beliefs about Haberman's Mid-Range Functions

Beliefs of Traditional Principals:	Mid-range Functions: Beliefs and Behaviors of Star Administrators	Beliefs of Star Principals:
Believe that principals must be responsive to district and state mandates	1. Leadership	S/he feels that principals must co-create and communicate a focused vision of student learning in chaotic times
The selection and assignment of teachers is best handled by human resources	2. Commitment to student learning	S/he believes that ineffective teachers must be removed at every cost
S/he may not understand why the 3 principles of unity of purpose, team building, or commitment to administrative tasks are principles or the relationship to school culture	3. Theory into Practice	Understand that principals operate by 3 principles; unity of purpose, team building and commitment to administrative tasks
Believe that social services are not a duty of the school	4. Role of the school serving children in poverty	Believe that students and families are connected to social services
S/he sees little to no role in improving teacher effectiveness and feels unaccountable for the results of teachers and learners.	5. Curriculum + Instructional Leadership	Believe that principals know and engage the curriculum; seek best instructional practices; know instructional strategies; and engage the academic life of the school
Does not recognize organizational and community pressures on the principal, staff, or students	6. Creating a positive school climate and fighting burnout	Are sensitive to demands made on him/her. They seek opportunities to celebrate and visitors, teachers, staff and learners feel safe, welcome, valued, and affirmed
Principals are in charge because they are smarter; they cannot conceive that a principal might be evaluate or offer creative criteria for	7. Evaluation/Accountability	Principals are the leaders because they understand they are culpable for progress and change
All decisions flow from the top, down	8. Decision making	Decision making must be shared
Leaders must never admit to their mistakes	9. Fallibility	Leaders must admit when they are wrong
Superintendents are served by the loyal principal, and principals are served by staff, teachers, parents and the community	10. Administrative style	Principals are servants to their stakeholders
Parents and community are roadblocks	11. Administrative relations with parents and community	Parents and the community are partners

defined and ingenious interviewing process, but it may accurately predict who will be successful administrators for children and youth in poverty.

GETTING THE PRINCIPAL INTERVIEW RIGHT

Haberman's aspiration to place a star principal in every school is based on the view that selection of the right principal is even more important than training. Principal development as a reform strategy is not succeeding in ways we all imagined. The programs in educational administration wrestle with rigor and quality (Creighton & Jones, 2001; Jackson & Kelley, 2002) and Darling-Hammond et al., (2007) surmise,

> no state we studied had yet assembled all the elements of a high-quality, finan-
> cially stable system for recruiting, preparing, and supporting the development
> of school leaders. Furthermore, based on our national survey, relatively few
> practicing principals across the country have regular opportunities for the
> kinds of support they find most useful to improving their practice. (p. 148)

The field of educational administration seeks innovative initiatives in an effort to redefine the goals and objectives of deteriorating programs (Mc-Carthy, 2002). Training programs for the principalship look to novel curriculum themes in management, educational entrepreneurship, substantive field experiences, and/or instructional leadership (Jackson & Kelley, 2002) that connect to an agreed upon knowledge base. Meanwhile, needy children do not have time for school leaders to train their way to competence.

The interview is a unique opportunity to fight against *selection blindness* with efforts to detect the most worthy principal candidates. There are various interview tools and protocols used by school districts in the selection of school executives. The interview process is rather standardized across school districts. Prospective candidates submit dossiers and their qualifications for the school opening are assessed. If s/he passes that hurdle, then s/he moves on to the all-important interview. Interviewers, with leadership checklists in hand, seek to establish if a candidate has the virtues and merits of a quality principal that mirror the ISCCL standards. The interview has served as the uncontested litmus test in determining an applicant's fitness as a principal.

The history of the principal interview is more than seven decades long and too voluminous for a fair critique in this chapter. An appraisal of the current interview surveys focus on knowledge, skills, and talent of the school leader critique. A quick Internet search leads any proactive candidate to find sample interview questions in preparation for the principal interview (see Table 5.2, *Traditional and Star Principals' Sample Responses to School Climate Interview Questions*). Table 5.2, for example, provides a microscopic probe into Haberman's mid-range functions for providing a positive

TABLE 5.2 Traditional and Star Principals' Sample Responses to School Climate Interview Questions

Sample Response of a Traditional Principal Candidate	Sample Interview Questions on School Climate	Sample Response of a Star Principal Candidate
I set the rules that are given to me and my expectations are that the staff will cooperate.	A. Describe ways you contribute to or facilitate collegial support and staff morale.	In order to build capacity for support, I would gather information from staff members and we decide as a team what will be best for teachers and students.
That the student understands there are consequences for bad behavior and disruptions will not be tolerated on my campus.	B. When dealing with a discipline problem with a student, what is your major concern?	The goal must be to determine as to why the student feels compelled to disrupt. I would act to find ways to learn more about the student and his life outside of school and always demonstrate respect to the student and parents upon contact so that they feel as though we are working in their best interest.
None. Teachers send me students that are disruptive, and I explain that we will not tolerate bad behavior. I will send them to alternative schools and get them out of the way of our teachers.	C. How much and what type of input do you solicit from a teacher in dealing with referrals and discipline problems with a student?	I have teams of teachers working together to research ways to build relationships with all teachers and students. I would let everyone know of our great expectations to deliver a message of care and concern for all students, and ensure they have opportunities to do their best in our school community. Students would always be included in the planning.

school climate—specific to the issue of discipline. The star principal shares responses that extend beyond predictable, rehearsed, and non-political banked reactions. Stars: institutionalize shared values on regulating punishment are accomplished when the principal takes the time to build capacity with students and teachers; seize the chance to explain that any disruptions are missed opportunities to teach learners and work feverishly to determine the root causes of discipline matters; and seek input from the family, community, staff, faculty, and the learners in finding solutions for discipline concerns. By contrast, the traditional principal concedes that: district rules are made to be followed; zero policies are inflexible; and giving up on disruptive students, or passing them through the system, is easier than investing time and supportive structures.

Beliefs, extracted from principals' interview responses, can accurately predict their attitudes and values and also give insight into how they will behave in schools. The HSASI studies have found that diagnostic and well-articulated selection interview questions are crucial for identifying quality principals who can build and sustain successful schools.

Research and Development of the HSASI[1]

The development of the HSASI questionnaire is the culmination of 50 years of research and development; merging research base with the most effective practices of star urban principals. The research and theory base was summarized in the 24 domains of the knowledge and skill base and laid out in *Principals for Our Changing Schools* published by The National Policy Board for Educational Administration.

Star urban principals in three great city school districts were identified: 27 in Houston, 18 in Milwaukee and 84 in Chicago. "Star" principals were invited to participate using the following criteria: achievement scores had risen in their schools for a three year period; they were rated by their faculties as effective instructional leaders; central office personnel identified them as accountable fiscal managers; and parents described them as effective in developing community support for their schools. These stars then engaged in a process of explaining their effective leadership behaviors. They participated in consensus building activities which involved grouping and ranking the performance functions which they believed constituted best practice and which they believed explained their success. The domains of the written knowledge base and the functions performed by the urban principals were then synthesized into 11 functions. This synthesis represents the functions that star urban teachers identified as their effective behaviors which can also be supported in the research literature.

Questions designed to assess the 11 functions of star urban principals were then developed to assess this synthesis of research and practice. In order to validate that the content of the questions dealt with the content they purported to be assessing, all the principals of the Milwaukee Public Schools in 2001 (167) were personally interviewed by Haberman over a period of 53 days. This process established content validity. Respondents, regardless of their level of administrative effectiveness, agreed that the questions dealt with the stated functions. The results of this study indicated that the effective functions cited by star principals were also supported in the literature and were indeed communicating common meanings to respondents. In addition, all question wordings that were ambiguous were clarified or discarded. In an ancillary study, 51 assistant principals were also interviewed. In spite of the fact that assistant principals were typically relegated to disciplinary duties, they identified 10 of the 11 functions on the questionnaire as explanations of star principals' effectiveness.

In addition to establishing content validity, this lengthy, in-depth process also provided a pool of responses to the same questions from principals deemed to be less than satisfactory as well as responses from star principals. Unsatisfactory or "failure" principals were those with attributes opposite to stars: their schools had declining achievement; they were not regarded as instructional leaders by their faculties; they were identified by central office administrators as "in trouble"; and they were not supported by their parents and communities. These were individuals in the process of retiring, being assigned principal coaches or being moved out of schools and reassigned.

As a result of these procedures, 11 functions representing sound theory and practice were developed into valid interview questions. Since our studies had included both stars and failure principals' responses it was also possible to score responses. The scores reflect the degree to which respondents' answers are closer to those made by star urban principals or to those made by failure principals to the same questions.

These procedures required one year to accomplish. At the conclusion of the year the questionnaire was taken back to the original three groups of star principals in Houston, Chicago and Milwaukee. The numbers of these groups had declined slightly (two less in Houston, one less in Milwaukee and eight less in Chicago). The star principals were asked to repeat the very same process they had engaged in initially; that is, they engaged in a process of consensus building in which they identified and ranked the behaviors they believed explained their effectiveness. The results of these activities indicated that the behaviors star urban principals had identified the previous year were the same ones they identified a year later. The second finding was that the answers of all the initial respondents' identified as stars were, in every case, closer to the star respondents identified in the Milwaukee sample than to the responses of the failing principals. The third finding confirmed that the questionnaire could be administered with inter-rater reliability; different interviewers scored respondents answers in the same ways.

CONCLUSION

There were three big ideas about principal selection from this chapter. First, the selection of school leaders requires a new perspective; one that moves us from *selection blindness* to selection astuteness. The role of the principalship, especially in hard to staff schools, is constantly being redefined by today's changing social and educational landscape. The vision of tomorrow's school leader is an archetype that is more community leader than CEO. Second, a star principal believes in one overarching philosophy—leadership for social justice. By examining the core of what principals believe, we can more accurately predict their effectiveness. Stars, when compared to their status quo counterparts, are principled and moral decision-makers fanatically focused on their stakeholders. Haberman asserts that star principals can be located by getting to the root of what they believe because administrative actions are dictated by one's core beliefs. Third the developmental approach for HSASI has yielded a questionnaire which synthesizes what the knowledge base indicates makes principals effective and what star urban principals themselves identify as explanations for their success. When this protocol was replicated one year later it yielded the same explanations of success. The interview questions developed from this synthesis have content validity for both star principals and failure principals. The scoring of respondents is reliable when used by various questioners who have been trained to use the interview.

HSASI users quickly come to understand that the star principal ideology is a value-laden system and no instrument, graduate study, or training can teach it; one either has a star principal ideology or you don't! The selection of better principals is too important to leave to chance. Let us use methods, like HSASI, that get it right for the sake of underserved learners. For Haberman, *better principals, better schools* is more than an axiom; it is a call to action to change the way American schools hire principals.

NOTE

1. Taken from Haberman, M. (2003, fall). The "star" principal selection interview. *The Haberman Newsletter, 8*(1) [available online]. Reproduced with permission.

REFERENCES

Beteille, T., Kalogrides, D., & Loeb, S. (2011). Stepping stones: Principal career paths and school outcomes. *Social Science Research, 41*, 904–919.

Bogotch, I. (2002). Educational leadership and social justice: Practice into theory. *Journal of School Leadership, 12,* 138–156.

Branch, G. F., Hanushek, E. A., & Rivkin, S. G. (2009). *Estimating principal effects.* Retrieved September 14, 2012, from http://www.urban.org/uploadedpdf/1001439-Estimating-Principal-Effectiveness.pdf

Browne-Ferrigno, T. (2003). Becoming a principal: Role conception, initial socialization, role-identity transformation, purposeful engagement. *Educational Administration Quarterly, 39*(4), 468–503.

Center for Public Education. (2012). *The principal perspective: Full report.* The National School Board Association. Retrieved from http://www.centerforpubliceducation.org/principal-perspective

Coelli, M., & Green, D. A. (2012). Leadership effects: School principals and student outcomes. *Economics of Education Review, 31,* 92–109.

Council of Chief State School Officers. (2008). *Interstate school leaders licensure consortium (ISLLC) standards for school leaders* [Electronic version]. Washington, DC: Author.

Creighton, T. B., & Jones, G. D. (2001). *Selection or self-selection? How rigorous are our selection criteria for education administration preparation programs?* Paper presented at the 2001 conference of the National Council of Professors of Educational Administration: Houston, TX. (ERIC No. ED 457 557)

Darling-Hammond, L., LaPointe, M., Meyerson, D., Orr. M. T., & Cohen, C. (2007). *Preparing school leaders for a changing world: Lessons from exemplary leadership development programs.* Stanford, CA: Stanford University, Stanford Educational Leadership Institute.

Davis, S., Darling-Hammond, L., LaPointe, M., & Meyerson, D. (2005). *Review of research. School leadership study. Developing successful principals.* Palo Alto, CA: Stanford Educational Leadership Institute.

Fenwick, L. T., & Pierce, M. C. (2001). The principal shortage: Crisis or opportunity? *Principal, 80*(4), 24–32.

Goldfarb, K. P., & Grinberg, J. (2002). Leadership for social justice: Authentic participation in the case of a community center in Caracas, Venezuela. *Journal of School Leadership, 12,* 157–173.

Haberman, M. (1999). *Star principals serving children in poverty.* Indianapolis, IN: Kappa Delta Pi.

Haberman, M. (2001). *The leadership functions of star principals serving children in poverty.* Houston, TX: The Haberman Educational Foundation.

Hallinger, P. (2015). The evolution of instructional leadership. In P. Hallinger & W. C. Wang (Eds.), *Assessing instructional leadership with the principal instructional management rating scale* (pp. 1–23). Sennweid, Switzerland: Springer International Publishing.

Hammond, J., Muffs, M., & Sciascia, S. (2001). The leadership crisis: Is it for real? *Principal, 81*(2), 28–32.

Jackson, B. L., & Kelley, C. (2002). Exceptional and innovative programs in educational Leadership. *Educational Administration Quarterly, 38*(2) 192–212.

Lortie, D. (2009). *School principal, managing in public.* Chicago, IL: University of Chicago Press.

Lovely, S. (2004). *Staffing the principalship: Finding, coaching, and mentoring school leaders.* Alexandria, VA: ASCD.

McCarthy, M. (2002). Educational leadership preparation programs: A glance at the past with an eye toward the future. *Leadership and Policy in Schools, 1*(3), 201–221.

McCarthy, M. (2005). How are school leaders prepared? Trends and future directions. *Educational Horizons, 77*(2), 74–81.

McCarthy, M., & Forsyth, P. B. (2009). *A historical review of research and development activities pertaining to the preparation of school leaders.* The Handbook of Research on the Education of School Leaders. Newberry Park, CA: SAGE.

Miller, A. (2013). Principal turnover and student achievement. *Economics of Education Review, 36*, 60–72.

Myung, J., Loeb, S., & Horng, E. (2011). Tapping the principal pipeline: Identifying talent for future school leadership in the absence of formal succession management programs. *Educational Administration Quarterly, 47*(5), 695–727.

NCES. (2014). *Condition of education 2014.* National Center for Education Statistics, U.S. Department of Education. Retrieved from http://nces.ed.gov/pubs2014/2014083.pdf

Orr, M. (2006). Mapping innovation in leadership preparation in our nation's schools of education. *Phi Delta Kappan, 87*(7), 492–499.

Pounder, D., Galvin, P., & Shepard, P. (2003). An analysis of the United States educational administrator shortage. *Australian Journal of Education, 47*(2), 133. Retrieved from http://www.questa.com/PM/qst?action. March 5, 2006.

Roza, M. (2003). *A matter of definition: Is there truly a shortage of school principals?* The Wallace Foundation. Retrieved from http://www.wallacefoundation.org/knowledge-center/school-leadership/state-policy/Documents/Is-There-Truly-a-Shortage-of-School-Principals.pdf

Schlechty, P. C. (2001). *Shaking up the school house: How to support and sustain educational innovation.* San Francisco, CA: Jossey-Bass Publishers.

Sergiovanni, T. J. (1996a). *Leadership for the schoolhouse: How is it different? Why is it important?* San Francisco, CA: Jossey-Bass Publishers.

Sergiovanni, T. J. (1996b). Leadership basics for principals and their staff. *Educational Forum, 60*, 267–270.

Sergiovanni, T. J. (1996c). *Moral leadership: Getting to the heart of school improvement.* San Francisco, CA: Jossey-Bass.

Sergiovanni, T. (2001). *The principalship: A reflective practice perspective* (4th ed.). Boston, MA: Allyn and Bacon.

Theoharis, G. (2007). Social justice educational leaders and resistance: Toward a theory of social justice leadership. *Educational Administration Quarterly, 43*(2), 221–258.

The Wallace Foundation. (2012). *The school principal as leader: Guiding schools to better teaching and learning.* Retrieved from http://www.wallacefoundation.org/knowledge-center/school-leadership/effective-principal-leadership/

Documents/The-School-Principal-as-Leader-Guiding-Schools-to-Better-Teaching-and-Learning.pdf

Waters, T., Marzano, R., & McNulty, B. (2004). Developing the science of educational leadership. *ERS Spectrum, 22*(1), 4–13.

ABOUT THE EDITORS

Delia Stafford

Known as the practitioner's practitioner, Ms. Delia Stafford is the President and CEO of The Haberman Educational Foundation, Inc. in Houston, TX and was named a 2015 *Elite American Educator*, a recognition for her achievements and leadership in developing educational programs for impoverished and at-risk youth. For nearly a decade, Ms. Stafford directed the nation's largest school district-based alternative teacher certification program in Houston Independent School District. She was twice recognized at White House ceremonies for her success in that program and her advocacy in finding good teachers for children at risk and in poverty. In addition to research interests in alternative teacher certification and teacher selection, Ms. Stafford's publications include urban school district-based teacher education, violence prevention, beliefs of effective teachers, student resilience, and research implementation. Ms. Stafford began The Haberman Educational Foundation in 1994 for the purpose of making visible and lasting improvements in the education of America's 15 million diverse children in poverty.

Valerie Hill-Jackson, EdD

Dr. Valerie Hill-Jackson received her Interdisciplinary Doctorate in Educational Leadership degree, summa cum laude, from St. Joseph's University in Philadelphia, Pennsylvania. She is a clinical professor in the Department of Teaching, Learning, and Culture at Texas A&M University and teaches in the Culture & Curriculum, Urban Education and Educational Leadership

Better Principals, Better Schools, pages 81–82

for Curriculum and Instruction online programs. She is also a Senior Researcher, a volunteer position, for the Haberman Educational Foundation. Dr. Hill-Jackson's research interests include: social justice leadership, service-learning and community education, ethnography, urban education, and gifted education.

Dr. Hill-Jackson has several book chapters to her credit and has written for peer-reviewed journals, including: *Multicultural Education Perspectives, Urban Education,* and *Kappa Delta Pi Record.* Hill-Jackson is the co-editor of *Transforming Teacher Education: What Went Wrong in Teacher Training and How We Can Fix It* (Stylus, 2010) and an internationally award winning educator and scholar. Early in her career, she received the prestigious American Educational Research Association/Spencer Fellowship and was conferred with the Lead Poisoning Star Award for her research in K–12 community education. In 2013, Hill-Jackson was conferred the Upton Sinclair Award and won a Traditional Core Fulbright Award.

ABOUT THE CONTRIBUTORS

Beverly E. Cross, PhD

Dr. Beverly Cross earned her doctorate in curriculum, instruction, and professional development from The Ohio State University. She is the Lillian and Morrie Moss Chair of Excellence in Urban Education at the University of Memphis. She provides leadership across the College of Education to prepare educational leaders with the knowledge and skills to enhance educational success for urban learners.

She is active at the national level and co-chaired the Urban and Equity Initiative for the Holmes Partnership that actively worked on equity, diversity and cultural competence in K–12 schools, higher education, and the education profession by recruiting, preparing, and sustaining faculty and students who reflect and deeply understand the implications of the rich diversity of cultural perspectives in this country. She also served on a National Education Association Indicators Advisory Panel to assist them in assuring their 3.2 million members meet the needs of *every* student particularly in diverse communities and schools.

Cross is nationally recognized for her record of teaching, research, scholarship, and service in urban education. She has conducted research in the areas of teacher diversity, urban education, multicultural and anti-racist education, and curriculum theory. She has written frequently on urban education, particularly issues of race, class, and culture in urban schools and achievement. Her research has appeared in such publications as the *Theory into Practice, Journal of Curriculum and Supervision, Education Leadership,* the *International Journal of Educational Reform* and the *Urban Review.* She edited a monograph entitled, *A Primer to Social Justice.*

Better Principals, Better Schools, pages 83–88
Copyright © 2016 by Information Age Publishing

Arthur "Gus" Jacob, EdD

Throughout his 40 years in education Gus Jacob has had a relentless focus on school improvement focusing on quality instruction through professional development and strong leadership. He currently teaches educational leadership at the University of Missouri–Kansas City and works as a leadership consultant with schools, districts, and states. His work in the Kansas City area and in the Midwest includes providing leadership training and leadership mentoring to several school districts. He is former director of the Missouri Education Policy Fellows Program in collaboration with the Institute for Educational Leadership in Washington, D.C. Additionally, Gus has 16 years of experience as an elementary and middle school principal, as well as serving in the role of Director of Professional Development for the Kansas City, Kansas Public Schools. He was selected principal of one of the 12 original Basic Schools in the nation working closely with Dr. Ernest Boyer. He is a certified trainer for the Haberman Educational Foundation focused on identifying "Star Teachers and Principals" for urban schools. Gus received his doctorate from the University of Kansas.

Jim Robins

Jim Robins has been involved in public education for almost 40 years. He has served as a classroom teacher and coach at both the middle school and high school levels and as a principal and assistant principal at both the middle and high school levels. Jim has 15 years of experience as a school superintendent in both Kansas and Missouri and has also worked as a consultant in various charter schools in the Kansas City area. Additionally, Jim has served for over 20 years as an adjunct professor, teaching various administrative classes at the graduate level. Jim's current position is as a professor at Baker University where he teaches a doctoral level course in ethics and advises doctoral students as they complete the dissertation process.

Jim and his wife Teresa are the parents of five children and three grandchildren. Teresa is a career kindergarten teacher with over 30 years of experience in the classroom. Jim and Teresa live in Kansas City, Missouri.

Jennifer Waddell, PhD

Jennifer Waddell, PhD is the Associate Director of the Institute for Urban Education at The University of Missouri–Kansas City. Her research interests include urban teacher preparation, multicultural education, and working with families and communities in urban teacher education. She is passionate about the selection, preparation, and retention of effective teachers and teacher leaders in urban schools. Recent publications include articles in

The Teacher Educator, Current Issues in Education, and *Multicultural Education.*
Dr. Waddell is an Associate Professor in the Division of Curriculum and
Instructional Leadership at UMKC.

Rodney E. Watson, PhD

Dr. Rodney E. Watson became Superintendent of the Spring Independent
School District in July 2014. Spring ISD serves over 36,000 prekindergarten
through twelfth-grade students in a diverse and growing district located
20 miles north of downtown Houston in an urban area of Harris County.
Prior to accepting the leadership role at Spring ISD, Dr. Watson served as
the Chief Human Resources Officer at the Houston Independent School
District, the largest district in Texas and the seventh-largest in the nation,
with more than 210,000 students and 30,000 employees supporting 276
area schools.

Dr. Watson received his PhD from the University of Missouri—Kansas City
in Urban Leadership and Policy Analysis in Curriculum and Instruction.
His professional affiliations include work with The Education Trust, the
Bill and Melinda Gates Foundation, the NAACP, the National Association
of Black School Administrators, and the American Counseling Association.

He has presented on a variety of topics to such diverse audiences as public school principals, Houston-area superintendents, the Texas State Sen-
ate Committee on Education, the U.S. House of Representatives Education
and Workforce Committee, the Council of the Great City Schools, the Bill
and Melinda Gates Foundation, and the National Urban League. Dr. Watson has also served as an adjunct professor of education at the University of
Missouri–Kansas City and the University of Texas–Austin.

Myra I. Whitney

Myra I. Whitney spent 37 years as a special education and elementary teacher
and principal, district principal cluster leader of 14 K–12 schools, elementary
academic superintendent of 37 schools, executive director of professional
development and associate superintendent of curriculum and professional
development leading learning for 16,000 employees. Myra mentors teachers
and principals to transform their schools. These experiences in leadership
encompassed change management, building staff capacity in instructional
improvement, and usage of Instructional Rounds in education through a
blended, coherent model of learning district initiatives. This work was driven
by the launch of a district comprehensive professional development plan and
policy. This expertise enabled her to establish and lead the development of
an aspiring leaders' leadership development program.

Myra has a continuous love for learning through her completion of Harvard's Public Education Leadership Project (PELP) and Instructional Rounds in Education and the Principal's Center, Learning Forward professional development academy and as a certified professional coach and master practitioner.

Announcing
Haberman Star Principal
Selection Interview Training!

Date: You Select
Place: Your District
Time: 8:00 – 4:30

The Haberman Educational Foundation. Inc.

"Selection is more important than training."
The Haberman Educational Foundation offers superintendents, principals, site-based teams and teacher leaders research-based strategies to select teachers and principals who will be unequivocally successful with students

---

No school can be better than the Principals and Teachers

For Four Decades, Dr. Haberman's
Research has Shown
that Principals Drive Student Achievement

1. The effect of school leadership is greater than student ethnicity, family income, school attended by students, or class size.

2. All groups of students benefit from effective principals that guide student learning.

Principals Who Succeed Know How to Build Relationships

If a principal candidate does not understand how to build relationships with teachers, students and their school community, it doesn't matter how much content knowledge experience, or credential strength they may offer.

The Haberman Star Principal Interview selects mature individuals who can build relationships with teachers, students and their school community

The scenario-based interview assesses qualities like persistence, stakeholder focus, ability to translate theory into practice, perception of at-risk behavior, and fallibility. Each component reflects an effective school correlation.

Dr. Martin Haberman is author of the acclaimed Kappa Delta Pi publication, STAR Principals Serving Children in POVERTY. All training participants receive his book and the interview tools which help to identify excellent principals.

To Schedule a Date,
Call 713-667-6185
or email us at d.staff@ix.netcom.com

Made in the USA
Coppell, TX
12 August 2020